THE INSIDER'S GUIDE TO HOME RECORDING

THE INSIDER'S GUIDE TO HOME RECORDING

RECORD MUSIC AND GET PAID

BRIAN TARQUIN

ALLWORTH PRESS
NEW YORK

Allworth Press books may be purchased in bulk at special discounts for sales promotion, corporate gifts, fund-raising, or educational purposes. Special editions can also be created to specifications. For details, contact the Special Sales Department, Allworth Press, 307 West 36th Street, 11th Floor, New York, NY 10018 or info@skyhorsepublishing.com.

15 14 13 12 11   5 4 3 2 1

Published by Allworth Press, an imprint of Skyhorse Publishing, Inc.

307 West 36th Street, 11th Floor, New York, NY 10018.

Allworth Press® is a registered trademark of Skyhorse Publishing, Inc.®, a Delaware corporation.

www.allworth.com

Cover design by Mary Belibasakis

Cover photo credit Erik Christian Photography

Library of Congress Cataloging-in-Publication Data is available on file

ISBN: 978-1-62153-445-7

Ebook ISBN: 978-1-62153-450-1

Printed in the United States of America

Table of Contents

Introduction

Nowadays, it's taken for granted that musicians have the option of recording their music at home. Affordable high-quality hardware and software tools designed for each step in the music production process are widely available. Choices abound, ranging from high-end to entry-level gear—often in portable packages, from laptops and 2-channel audio interfaces all the way down to pocket-sized digital recorders and smartphones running basic recording apps. Opportunities for musicians to produce their own (and their friends' or clients') musical projects are most definitely out there.

At the start of the twenty-first century, many manufacturers of professional audio products took a growing interest in developing budget-priced products for home-based end-users, to give them an entry point. Thanks largely to advances in technology combined with falling prices, personal studios of all sizes and budget levels, great and small, have become commonplace across the broader musical landscape as the home recording market continues to expand. And professional, full-time mixing and mastering engineers working in personal and commercial facilities now receive a sizeable percentage of their projects from musicians who record at home.

Home recording studios are nothing new, of course; they have existed in some form or another for decades. Les Paul experimented at home with tape and audio equipment, and pioneered the concept of multi-track recording in 1949. Sir Paul McCartney famously produced his 1970 debut solo album, *McCartney*, at home using a four-track Studer tape machine. But I think the current proliferation of personal studios belonging to working and hobbyist musicians traces its roots to the late 1970s when the Tascam PortaStudio four-track cassette recorder was introduced.

It's been an exciting ride for me in witnessing and experiencing the evolution of the personal studio market since I entered a home studio for the first time in 1986. I'm privileged to have learned and written about music production since 1998 through interviews with artists, engineers, and producers as a staff editor for *Music & Computers, Electronic Musician*, and, since 2006, *Mix* magazine.

Several years ago, while working for *Mix*, I discovered the work and career of this book's author, Brian Tarquin. A multiple Emmy Award–winner for his music composition and direction, Brian has appeared in the pages of *Mix*, as well as other respected music and audio magazines, numerous times to discuss his varied endeavors. I was immediately impressed and inspired by a story about his Bohemian Productions label, which I proofread for *Mix*'s April 2007 issue. He talks in clear detail about how he designed his personal studio, Jungle Room Studios (which at that time was located in Nyack, New York), incorporating both analog and digital equipment to accommodate a fast-paced workflow to best handle tight deadlines for TV and album projects. I liked his ideas and philosophy, and became a fan of his work from that point forward. I also think that his foundation as a guitarist in pursuit of the best possible sounds and tones served him well when he expanded his interests into engineering and producing.

Later on, I interviewed Brian about sessions for his album *Les Paul Dedication: Guitar Masters Vol. 3 & 4* (2010), and then about the launch of his online production music library, TV Film Trax, and the design and construction of his current Jungle Room Studios inside a two-hundred-year-old house on a farm in the Catskills in upstate New York (2012). In each story, Brian very informatively describes his thought process behind his work: how he strategized the transformation of the farm house into a comfortable, pleasant, and highly efficient studio environment; his "old-school" preference for recording to analog gear, and the ways in which he interfaces digital audio workstations like Pro Tools and Logic with tape; how he sets up a rhythm section in his tracking room; his microphone choices and placements, and how they affect the mix down the road; the interaction of microphones, amplifiers, and room; the differences between recording an instrumental guitar album and producing cues for TV or film.

Because Brian is so thorough, thoughtful, passionate, and engaging when it comes to sharing his knowledge—and because of the wisdom he gained through his experiences in music over more than twenty years—I was excited when I learned that he had written *The Insider's Guide to Home Recording*. As a musician who started working in commercial studios in the '80s, learned to be an engineer on analog gear at a recording school just as digital equipment was being introduced, and then went on to build three top-notch personal studios and a multifaceted successful freelance career, Brian is in a perfect position to help you understand how best to choose, set up, and use your own studio space.

And he understands that musicians are creative people who don't want to get bogged down with excessive technical details that take time away from the music. *The Insider's Guide to Home Recording* gets down to business and covers the most essential topics, from start (selecting the right space) to finish (mixing)—with vital information in between about choosing equipment, understanding the engineer's role and the producer's role, and recording techniques.

As with music production equipment, there are many choices out there when it comes to books about building and recording in home studios. I invite you to jump into *The Insider's Guide to Home Recording* and enjoy the journey.

Matt Gallagher
Mix magazine
June 2014

Foreword

The home recording industry has become such a lucrative business for pro audio manufacturers in the past two decades. In the past, it was berated with a tsunami of harsh criticism and insults, something not to be taken seriously. But this all changed when, in the early '90s, we started seeing the digital revolution creep into our lives. Things like the DAT recorders (Digital Audio Tape), ADAT (Alesis Digital Audio Tape), and the Tascam DA-88. These were digital multi-track recording devices that used various size cartridges to record music digitally. The ADAT used the VHS tape that was very popular in the '80s to record and watch movies on, where the DA-88 used the smaller cartridge format like the Hi8 used on camcorders. The DAT format was a two-track mix down format, whereby the ADAT and DA-88 were eight-track format, in which you could hook up to three machines together to achieve twenty-four multi-track recording. This was the dawn of a new age and from that point on everything progressed until we reached today's standards of computer hard drive recording.

But regardless of the format, home recording has always been the preference for many artists. Recording from home gives the artist the creative flexibility and freedom to work at their own pace. Look at Tom Scholz from the band Boston, recording in his basement studio the band's initial demos of "More Than a Feeling," "Peace of Mind," "Rock and Roll Band," and "Something About You," which garnered a deal with Epic Records. In those days, record companies were hung up on re-recording demos in large studios, but with the insistence of Scholz, the album was recorded in his basement studio and mixed in Los Angeles at a commercial studio. How about other classic albums recorded in home studios, like *Exile on Main Street* by The Rolling Stones, *The Downward*

Spiral by Nine Inch Nails, *Nebraska* by Bruce Springsteen, *OK Computer* by Radiohead, *Hounds of Love* by Kate Bush, and the list goes on.

Having been born in the '60s during the overlapping generations of the baby boomers and Gen X, I grew up with analog recording tape in all of its facets: reel to reel, eight-track, cassettes, carts, etc. I was raised in New York City, a town alive with music clamoring from a plethora of clubs like Max's Kansas City, The Peppermint Lounge, The Ritz, The Lone Star Café, and The Bottom Line. My dad, Perry J. Browne, a good Irishman from Concord, Mass., had been a radio personality in the '40s and '50s who worked with the Bob & Ray Show and Robert Taylor, the film star. I remember he used to record all sorts of voice-over tapes in the house with his booming baritone voice. There was a quarter-inch four-track Grundig reel-to-reel tape recorder that was just calling my name, great for recording multiple guitar parts. I always thought it was so cool to sit in that sunroom and be able to hear the tracks played back, and to physically cut and edit the parts with a razor-blade and edit block.

Since the turn of the century, the world has seen an explosion in the home recording market. Twenty-five years ago, the pro audio marketplace was a very different world. Music stores didn't have pro audio sections like they do today; you had to go to specialty stores, like Coast Recording in Los Angeles, to buy recording equipment. Even the so-called "affordable" equipment by manufacturers like Tascam and Fostex was extremely expensive. Reel-to-reel players were the only game in town for recording, and to buy a machine from one of the large manufactures like Otari, Studer, and MCI was like buying a house. These twenty-four-track, two-inch machines were between fifty and seventy-five thousand, and what most studio owners did was lease them by bank financing—much like leasing a car today. No computers, no plug-ins, no auto tuning, no bouncing to disk; you had to be on your game as both an engineer and a player. Sure, you could punch-in, but I've been in sessions where the engineer missed the punch out and accidentally erased the next bar of the song. As an engineer back then, you really felt like you were a part of the music because you were constantly watching the meters, writing down times off of the tape player, adjusting thresholds on the compressor. It was really a group effort to get a good recording, and it was so important to have a good assistant working the control room with you. I must say, you can hear the difference in those albums from those big recording days of yesteryear.

However, with the digital revolution, we have more recording flexibility. If we miss a punch today in Pro Tools, all we do is hit undo, and *voila*, everything is back. With this new technology comes affordability, which for the home recording market is key. I remember when "Sound Tools" came out in the early '90s, amazing us all with waveform editing (only in stereo). Very expensive for the time, but it paved the way for all of the hard drive recording programs out today like Logic and Pro Tools. I remember being a young musician in the '80s having to save up money to buy enough studio time to record a three-song demo. Hell, that's why I went to audio engineering school, so I could learn the equipment and be able to record my own music cheaply during downtime at a studio where I was working.

With today's standards, we have all of the technology we need at our fingertips. No wonder there is an explosion of home recording studios. This book is a simple guide, perfect for both the novice and the most experienced musicians. I wanted to make this book an easy read and not get into a technical handbook of the theory of sound and physics. Simply use your *ears*! Other reference books seem to obsess with the standards and common practices. *Forgettaboutit!* This is a creative field, there is no one way to mix, like there is no one way to compose a song.

The book begins with choosing the right space for a studio set and a breakdown of some of the Digital Audio Workstations (DAW) that are widely used in the business today. The book will also encourage experimentation and go over cool tricks and tips on getting better recordings. Pro Tools and Logic will be addressed thoroughly and we will talk about how analog tape can warm up mixes. Importantly, there is a chapter that examines the role of both engineer and producer and how they interact with musicians. This is key because you have to know when a song is finished and what equipment you may need for the mix to get a favorable end result. For instance, I really learned to make good records in London during the '90s recording my solo records for Instinct records. The producer was also the engineer, and by watching him, I saw how he walked the thin line between the two jobs. It's always easier to have a designated engineer and a separate producer because as an artist, you want to just concentrate on your performance. But by having a home studio, you learn how to be all three—artist, producer, and engineer—and with time you know when you've got the best performance, out of yourself as well as hired musicians. Communication is paramount in achieving a good working relationship with the musician and when you are both the producer and the engineer.

This can be overwhelming at first, right out of the gate, but as with everything, the more experience you get under your belt the better judgment you develop. I want the book to guide home recording users through the steps of tracking and familiarizing themselves with not only the newest plug-ins, but also the classic gear that might be extremely useful for your projects. Keep in mind, recording and mixing is super fun and can be one of the greatest and most creative endeavors a musician can take on. John Lennon and Paul McCartney loved the recording process so much that they stopped touring altogether, opting for making records.

Chapter 1

Building the Foundation

Think of creating a studio space similar to building a house—the foundation is paramount! What good is a beautiful house built on a weak foundation or on a soft marshy area in the middle of an open field? I'll tell you one thing: once the foundation is compromised, it is all over! A perfect example is the Tappan Zee Bridge, which has been a part of my life as a New Yorker from birth. They decided to build it over the widest point of the Hudson River with less than standard material. It is so bad that the History Channel dubbed it one of the most dangerous bridges in America on their special "The Crumbling of America." It has become known as the "hold your breath bridge"; hope you make it across before it collapses. Well, the same goes for building a workspace for music—the shape of the room, the wall and ceiling reflection, electrical setup, floor material, etc. are all foundations. Don't get me wrong, you certainly don't need to have an architect design your room, but awareness of these things is good before diving into it. Of course, with today's technology, you don't need as much space as studios did in the past, but the same basic sound reinforcement applies if you plan on not using headphones all of the time.

If you've been down this road before or you are thinking about creating the perfect recording space, I've got some helpful step-by-step tips to make your space work for you. First, if you've browsed your local bookstore, you will find that there are a plethora of books on the subject, as well as numerous opinions on what issues to prioritize first. The considerations are endless, from studio size to acoustical treatment to wall panels, absorbers, and diffusers, to spacing of glass, sound reinforced doors, floating walls, ceilings and floors, to blah, blah, blah. But the first and foremost important aspect is the *electrical!* No matter how much money you spend on your design, whether it is a large professional studio or a small eight-by-eight room, do not overlook the importance of setting up the receptacles and lights before the wall goes up. Believe me, I learned this the hard way when I built my first studio. The wrong electrical setup can cause an irritating, persistent hum that goes through the board and ultimately to your recordings. I ask you, what good is using a SSL, Neve, or even a Trident Recording Console when the sound quality is stifled? Ground loops are the most common problem in home studios, as well as that nasty light noise that feeds itself from wall dimmers. Having built a number of studios and grappled with this common problem with grounding noise, I took a journal and a digital camera to record the process on one of my builds.

BUILDING THE RIGHT SPACE

On this particular project, we were dealing with one large open space, so we needed to create a control room with a separate live room. The room had thirteen-foot ceilings, so we had to figure out a creative and affordable way of dividing the space. So I started by breaking the room in two halves, and at the narrowest point between walls, I built an eight-foot wall (Fig. 1.1). First, I framed it out with two-by-sixes at a height of eight feet.

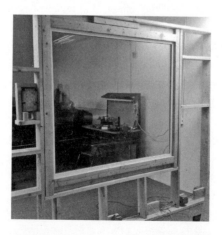

Figure 1.1 Eight-foot studio wall frame with double pane four-by-six glass window

Figure 1.2 Powerstat dimmer mounted on the frame before insulation

Once it was framed out, I mounted the Powerstat wall box in the control room and mounted the orange receptacles both in the live room and the control room (fig 1.2). We also brought in a double paned four-by-six window for the control room, which looked out into the live room, and placed it within the wall frame (fig 1.3).

Figure 1.3 Double pane four-by-six glass window mounted onto the wood frame before insulation

Figure 1.4 Enclosed outlet mounted on wood frame

Figure 1.5 Inside outlet showing isolated ground to prevent hums or ground loops from external sources

Then our trusty electrician came in and wired everything back to the box, outlets, dimmer, and track lights (figs. 1.4 and 1.5). Now it was time to finish the wall. To contain the noise factor, we used mounting sound board, which you can find at Home Depot or Lowe's, and nailed those directly on to the frame (fig. 1.6). Once the frame was completely covered, we added a nice knotty pine wood to add warmth to the space (figs. 1.7 and 1.8).

Figure 1.6 Soundboard attached to the wood frame of two-by-fours helps absorb sound

Figure 1.7 Tarquin using an air gun to nail the knotty pine boards to the frame

Figure 1.8 Final knotty pine finish and trim to window adds finishing touches

As for the door that fits between the live room and the studio, we used a heavy single swing three-by-seven acoustical door fitted with a small window purchased from Acoustical Solutions (fig. 1.9). The door's STC (Sound Transmission Classification) ratings are available from STC 41 up to STC 57. What's great about Acoustical Solutions is that they also make custom doors, as well as over-sized doors, undersized doors, double doors, swinging doors, tandem doors, and doors with or without windows. You will also need a reliable door jamb seal that fits above the door to the wall. They make an acoustical seal, which features a unique compress-o-matic design with a sound-absorbing neoprene rubber gasket that compresses to form a tight seal as the door is closed. The door jamb seals include adjusting screws for field correction of irregular clearances that might otherwise compromise the sound performance. This ensures a tight seal for the door, and the adjust feature is useful in future adjustments (fig. 1.10).

Figure 1.9 Acoustical Solutions door mounted on wall frame with Powerstat dimmer

Figure 1.10 Studio door has an adjustable seal on the bottom and a sound-absorbing neoprene rubber gasket

Figure 1.11 Finished studio door with knotty pine surface and trim

Figure 1.12 Finished door and window with flush mounted Powerstat dimmer

After that, we had to address the five feet of space between the top of the frame and the ceiling (fig. 1.13). I wanted something that would be lighter and more flexible, so we didn't have to build another heavy wall. So I framed it with two-by-fours and used an acoustical treatment made by the company Acoustical Solutions. The product is called AlphaSorb™ Barrier Fabric Wrapped Wall Panels, consisting of Audio-Seal™ Sound Barrier with the addition of the sound barrier septum. These panels offer an outstanding STC rating of twenty-nine combined with an NRC rating of 0.85–1.05, which is a good bang for the buck, plus they can customize the size of the panels. The fabric wraps a one-inch fiberglass with a sheet of sound barrier vinyl in between the layers of fiberglass. We used a nail gun and got the panels up quickly (figs. 1.14 and 1.15).

Figure 1.13 Upper part of the wall framed with two-by-fours and anchored to the walls on each side

Figure 1.14 Final AlphaSorb™ Barrier Fabric Wrapped Wall Panels, consisting of AudioSeal™ Sound Barrier

Figure 1.15 The outer wall with the AlphaSorb™ Barrier Fabric Wrapped Wall Panels

CONTROL ROOM ACOUSTICS

This is the room where everything goes down. This is where you'll live, both to track and mix, so it's got to be right. In the control room area, we were dealing with cement walls, so this made it a little harder to manage concerning walls. So I built a floating wall system framed with two-by-fours, making sure to angle all of the corners (fig. 1.16). The frames were then fastened with cement wall screws at strategic places to hold the frame tightly in place (fig. 1.17). I then took more panels of the AlphaSorb™ Barrier Fabric Wrapped Wall Panels and placed them on the outside frame side by side and screwed the panels in place (fig. 1.18). This designated wall was where we placed the Trident mixing console. Because we were dealing with a space with high ceilings and a lot of cement, we also hung a few heavy-duty Oriental rugs on the back wall to absorb some of the reflection from the monitors and slapback from side to side.

Figure 1.16 Two-by-four frame attached to the cement wall for the absorption panels

Figure 1.18 Wall frame with an AlphaSorb™ Barrier Fabric Wrapped Wall Panel

Figure 1.17 Two-by-fours fastened with cement wall screws to hold the frame tightly to the wall

Figure 1.19 Finished wall with AlphaSorb™ Barrier Fabric Wrapped Wall Panels

11

One of the largest undertakings was dealing with the ceiling. Since it was thirteen feet tall with exposed beams and insulation, we had to find a way to control the sound for mixing, yet leave some of the openness of the space exposed. I opted to design a large angled sound reflector (eight-by-eight) that would be installed only above the mixing console. I started out by building a stand-alone frame using two-by-fours. I then secured the top of the hanging frame to the wood beams on the ceiling and the bottom of the frame to the cement wall at a ninety-degree angle (fig. 1.20). Because of the thirteen-foot ceilings, it was a bit tricky, but with a twelve-foot ladder, a power miter saw, and cement screws, I got the frame secured. The next issue to tackle was what material to cover the frame with. I decided to use a quarter inch of plywood with the pine furring across in rows, to ensure evenness. Once the basic framing of the reflector was done, I chose two sheets of composite board measuring four by eight, which I cut into four quarters each, and glued four Auralex two-by-two squares to each of the panels (figs. 1.21, 1.22, and 1.23). This made it a lot easier to lift each one to the frame and then fasten. For the top pieces, we had to use a pulley device so we could hold them in place while we screwed in the panels. The Auralex foam had to be pulled back a few inches so we could place the screws directly to the plywood onto the frame, so as not to tamper with the look of the foam.

Figure 1.20 Two-by-fours making up the basic frame for the overhead reflector

Figure 1.21 Ceiling frame with a covering of composite boards

Now there was a question of the back wall. This was made of wood and was a straight shot up to the ceiling. As I mentioned earlier, we hung two rugs on the back wall but they were only five-by-seven each. So I fabricated diamond-shaped wall treatments to be hung in strategic places in the room. I used twelve two-by-threes and three sheets of four-by-eight Luan board. What is Luan? It is a quarter-inch sheet of plywood veneer board, the same material typically used in kitchens or bathrooms. I took four two-by-twos and framed the two-by-threes around to fit, then placed the Luan plywood underneath as a base. I made three of these traps, placing two on the back wall about nine feet up and spaced about seven feet apart, and hung the last one on the perpendicular wall on the left, above the AlphaSorb™ Barrier Fabric Wrapped Wall Panels. Aesthetically, they looked great, and they worked great at absorbing sound, so we built three more of these traps and placed them in the live room as well.

13

Figure 1.22 Auralex two-by-two squares glued to the composite board

Figure 1.23 Finished large angled sound reflector (eight-by-eight)

CLEAN ELECTRICITY

Ground loops are created by improperly designed or improperly installed equipment and are a major cause of noise and interference in audio and video systems. They can also create an electric shock hazard, which we guitarists know all too well. Have you ever played through an old Fender amp and the ground switch on the back is accidentally turned off, and you touch the guitar strings and a piece of metal on the amp—*zap!* Thank you very much for that! Well, same idea. For instance, if two pieces of audio equipment are plugged into different power outlets, there will often be a difference in their respective ground potentials. If a signal is passed from one to the other via an audio connection with the ground wire intact, this potential difference will cause a spurious current through the cables, generating an audible buzz. You get this with certain keyboard workstations as well, so guys use a ground lifter—that little orange plug that has no ground prong on the end. Use it on everything, so as to dodge that surprising shock, especially if you are ground lifting audio equipment. The best way to eliminate this problem is use ground isolated reciprocals (fig. 1.24). I highly recommend that you use a licensed electrician to install them; not cheap, but your recordings depend on it. You should use only these orange receptacles for your studio equipment to ensure no unwanted hums. Otherwise, there's a good chance of getting feedback noise from that microwave or mini refrigerator nearby in your mixes. I have worked in studios where a sudden surge from the microwave caused this crazy buzzing sound in the audio during a session. It always struck me as funny when guys worried about the microphone placement, but never addressed the obvious electrical hums buzzing all around their studios.

Figure 1.24 Ground isolated reciprocals to isolate unwanted hum and noise

15

LIGHTING

Now it's time to address the lighting issues. If you are like many musicians who like to record under dim lights, you'll need to invest in what is called "incandescent lighting controls." What the hell is that? Well, it is a light control extensively used for incandescent lighting in residential, theatrical, institutional, commercial, and industrial installations. These dimmers are continuously adjustable transformers that control light intensity by controlling the voltage applied to the lamps. Basically, it offers a smooth performance with no audio or video interference. If you use a cheap three-dollar dimmer from Home Depot, as you dim the lights there will be horrible noise interference in the audio. Superior Electric makes these wall dimmer boxes called "Powerstat." Professional recording studios around the world house several of these units in their facilities. The bad news is they are very expensive, but very necessary. I paid $500 for mine at the time. The good news is that after spending money on those babies, we were able to then buy some affordable track lights for the remaining bare walls (fig. 1.25).

Figure 1.25 Track lighting mounted on the wall above the AlphaSorb™ Barrier Fabric Wrapped Wall Panel

Figure 1.26 Recording light mounted in the door frame above the studio door

Figure 1.27 Finished wall with Powerstat dimmer

After all these years of moving and being a gypsy, I finally developed my own portable four-foot rack, equipped with orange isolated outlets and a Powerstat dimmer, both with twist lock connection to hook up to any breaker box (figs. 1.28-1.31).

Figure 1.28 Powerstat dimmer mounted in portable rack

Figure 1.29 Four-foot rack housing orange isolated ground outlets and Powerstat dimmer

Figure 1.30 Back of the rack with isolated ground outlet

Figure 1.31 Three self-contained orange outlets mounted in the front of the portable rack

CONCLUSION

I must say, every time I embark on building a new studio, I learn so much more about the way sound works within its confines and how it travels. If you would like to delve further into building your own space, some good reference books to check out are *Sound Studio Construction on a Budget* by F. Alton Everest and *Home Recording Studio, Build It Like the Pros* by Rod Gervais. Through trial and error, I've learned that no matter the dimensions of your studio, most importantly the space has to be comfortable and conducive to your needs. You can always address any harsh or bad reflected areas in the room with acoustical wall treatment. I've been in studio control rooms and wondered how in the world the engineer could mix, with so many crazy reflections and structural interference scattered throughout the room.

This brings me back to my early days of recording my first two albums in London as a solo artist for Instinct. The producer had the most unusual recording studio nestled in the attic of an old brownstone. The space was crammed and the ceilings were low. I could barely stand up straight, so I did all of my recordings sitting down in the control room where the producer sat. It was like being in a tree fort with low hanging eves and a slanted window that overlooked smoke stack roofs down Colney Hatch Lane. But what went through my mind the whole time was, "How in the world can anyone mix in a room like this?" I didn't stay there for the mixes, but when we heard the final production they were fantastic! In fact, the album went on to chart Top Ten at Radio and Top Forty on Billboard. But he did record the CD on an Otari 90 twenty-four-track analog machine through a Neve console. So, at the end of the day, I really believe it's your *ears* that really produce the best sound, because the best engineers can mix a great record in an empty swimming pool. Don't get trapped by all of these high-end pro audio sites trying to sell you $6,000 control windows, because it's not what you spend, it's how you use it!

Chapter 2

Setting Up Your Studio

When you are contemplating gear to set up your studio, the types of productions you intend to record can usually narrow it down. For example, if you are a keyboardist and plan on doing comprehensive MIDI recording with solely composing in mind, then you might want to go with MOTU's Digital Performer. Or if you plan on editing as a main function, Pro Tools may be the way to go. However, if you plan on recording live metal bands, you might want to think about a combination of Pro Tools and analog recording, such as reel-to-reel tape. Why? Well, there is such a thing called "tape saturation" and it affects each instrument differently. Drums and bass are affected most notably by such saturation, which gives the fatter/fuller analog sound to them. So what some people do today, myself included, is use the best of both worlds, analog and digital. So you can choose to record drums and bass on a two-inch analog sixteen- or twenty-four-track format and then transfer it over to your DAW, and continue to record other parts digitally. We'll take a look at the pros and cons of such choices in this chapter.

CHOOSING THE RIGHT DAW

The basic concept of every DAW on the market today is generally the same, which can be used with any user interface. These systems are based on multi-track tape recorder layouts, which obviously made it much easier for old school guys like me to adapt easily, coming from analog recording. The standard layout on DAWs is to have a transport control with play, rewind, record, etc., waveform editing as well as individual track controls on a mixer with moving faders, and the capability for using plug-in software on each track.

Interestingly enough, the first version of a DAW was from a company called Soundstream in 1977, which created a system they called "The Digital Editing System." It was made up of a mini computer that took a fourteen-inch platter hard disk drive and a storage oscilloscope to display audio waveforms. It had its own display monitor and analog to digital converters called DAI, or Digital Audio Interface. It could do the same kind of crossfades and waveform editing we find today on every household computer. The price factor held it back because of expensive storage devices and its slow processing power due to the technology of the time.

Figure 2.1 Pro Tools 11 HD

DIGIDESIGN PRO TOOLS

Fast-forward a decade into the '80s and consumer computer companies like Apple Macintosh, Atari ST, and the Commodore Amiga started to show more promise. It was two unemployed graduates from the University of California, Berkeley, with electrical engineering backgrounds, Evan Brooks and Peter Gotcher, who ironically started Pro Tools. They had developed the software Sound Designer in 1984, which was originally used to edit drum sample sounds for the E-mu Emulator keyboard. But then in 1989, a company called Digidesign launched a software program called "Sound Tools" specifically made for Apple computers. This directly brought in the beginning of modern DAW, though at the time was solely two-track editing. Then in 1991, they offered a four-track recording system for thousands of dollars, and moved on in 1994 to Pro Tools III with sixteen- to forty-eight-tracks. Today we are up to Pro Tools 11 (fig. 2.1), boasting the first sixty-four-bit Pro Tools application that is compatible with interface hardware on the market other than their own. In the short thirty-year history of the company, it has come a long way both in technology and price.

Figure 2.2 A typical Pro Tools edit window view

Figure 2.3 A typical Pro Tools mix window view

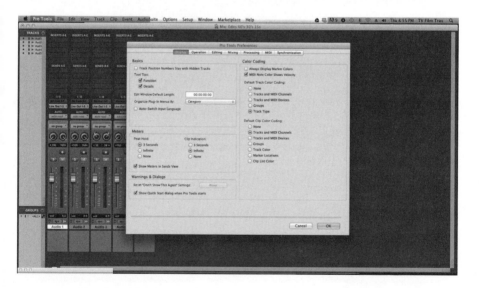

Figure 2.4 Pro Tools preference screen

Through its history, Pro Tools has always been a closed-format system, meaning you could only use their software with their specific hardware. However, with the release of Pro Tools 9 they had to change their controlling attitude with the ever-biting, encroaching market share of other more flexible companies. This is very similar to Apple succumbing to the success of Intel in PC computers, to the point of having no choice but incorporating Intel into Apple. Hence with Pro Tools 9 came the freedom of choosing your own hardware interface and not being stuck with the monopoly of Pro Tools pricey hardware. Well done, Avid Audio! Another welcome change was being able to authorize via an iLok device. Before, you had to actually register Pro Tools to your computer and get those ridiculous authorization codes. Now when you update to another computer or even use various computers, the authorization is in the iLok itself, not the computer you are using. Basically, an iLok is a USB device to register protected software (fig. 2.5); you create your own *iLok ID* so that the software license can be deposited in your iLok.com user account (fig. 2.6). The wonders of the modern age!

Figure 2.5 Typical iLok to register protected software

Figure 2.6 www.iLok.com license manager page

Since Pro Tools was one of the first, it became industry standard for recording studios, music editing, postproduction, and all forms of music production by the twenty-first century. However, the competition has been right on their heels in recent years, which was one of the reasons Avid had to make Pro Tools compatible with other manufacturers' hardware interfaces. But for me, Pro Tools is a like an old friend because it was the first digital platform I learned and I can easily edit and mix on it. Really, there is no difference between any of the other platforms and Pro Tools, other than the subtle positioning of the tools and their icons. It comes down to what feels most comfortable for your workflow. I've used Logic, which I like a lot, Digital Performer, which I don't care for, Reason, and other platforms out there; it is all the same basic structure of waveform editing and virtual mixing.

I think because Pro Tools was one of the first on the market and feels the most intuitive, it has always remained a favorite for industry people like myself. Additionally, coming from the days of "Sound Tools," it is a natural progression with the same company. The thing to keep in mind with Pro Tools is that when you bounce to disk, it achieves it in real time, meaning it will play the song at normal speed from beginning to end when you want to bounce the track to hard drive regardless of the file format (figs. 2.7 and 2.8).

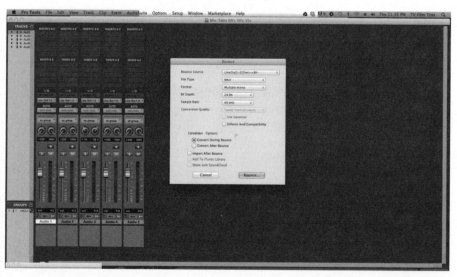

Figure 2.7 Pro Tools "bounce" menu

Figure 2.8 Pro Tools "bounce" menu choose file format

APPLE/LOGIC

The music program Logic was originally developed in the '90s by C-Lab, a music software company in Germany. C-Lab later became the Emagic Company, which Apple acquisitioned in 2002.

Figure 2.9 Logic Express 8 version page

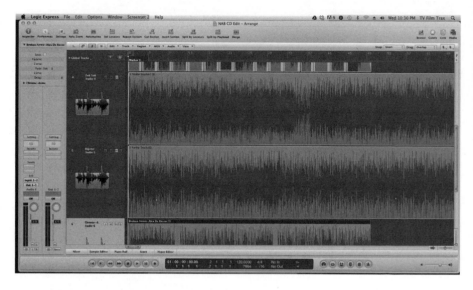

Figure 2.10 Logic Express 8 edit page view

Logic was a direct evolution from the software Creator that was developed in the late '80s for the Atari ST computer. As the program developed, it became Notator, which was a linear MIDI sequencer that could give musical notation. Very much like drum machines that would later be developed like the Akai MPC series, the sequencer was based on writing patterns. So you would have sixteen tracks per pattern that would make up each part of the song— intro, verse, chorus, middle-eight break, and so forth. Hence, you would build your song by arranging each pattern at a given point to form the final song. This became the basis for MIDI sequencing through the next twenty-five years and is still used in sequencing on keyboard workstations. At this time, Notator's biggest rival was Steinberg's Cubase, which offered the alternative track-based sequencing, as opposed to pattern-based. So in 1993 C-Lab programmers made an exodus from the company to form Emagic. They renamed the software Notator Logic, desperately trying to intergrade pattern-based sequencing with track-based recording. As the Atari platform became obsolete, they embraced the new and upcoming Mac platform and found a match made in heaven.

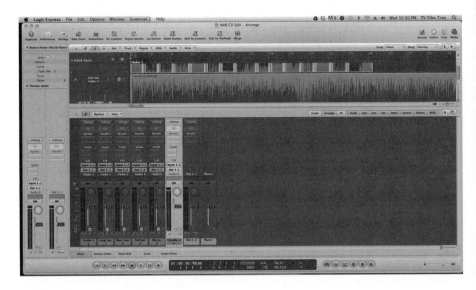

Figure 2.11 Logic mix window view

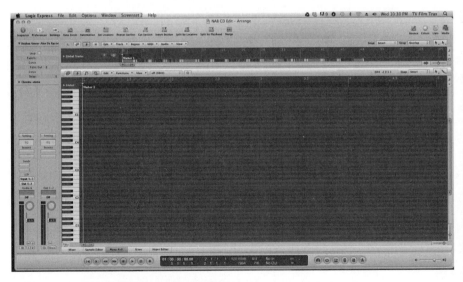

Figure 2.12 Logic MIDI sequence window view

I always found Logic very intuitive and easy to use. There are never issues with the operating system because it is made especially for the Mac.

It is an open system so you can use hardware systems like Motu, Focusrite, or even Digidesign 002 with no problems. Although I like Pro Tools, the same cannot be said about it. There is always a driver situation when you upgrade to another computer (drivers are installed in a current operating system so the program can operate correctly with the computer) and until recently, you were stuck with Avid interfaces. I believe this is why Avid had to finally come out with an open Pro Tools system that could play nice with other hardware devices. Another great Logic feature is the flexible bouncing capabilities, so you can "bounce to disc" offline, meaning not having to listen to the whole song in real time. It allows you to bounce in a fraction of the time without losing any of the audio quality, and has a great MIDI sequencer. Pro Tools, on the other hand, has one of the most archaic MIDI sequencers, which is a bit clumsy and awkward to use. It is a fantastic editor and mixer, but falls short for MIDI users. If you plan on using a platform for mainly MIDI sequencing or MIDI recording, I would steer clear of Pro Tools and go with a program like Logic. The rest has basically all the same features as Pro Tools, just different names for tools and their placement on the screen.

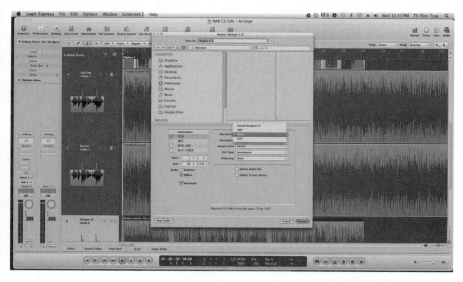

Figure 2.13 Logic bounce window enables a choice of sample rate, resolution, etc.

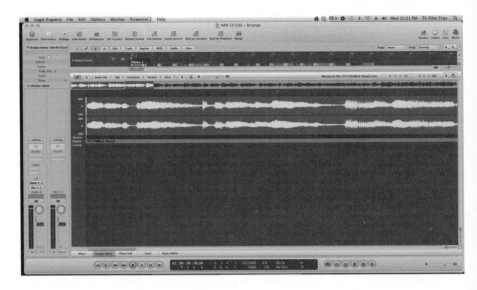

Figure 2.14 Logic sample editor window

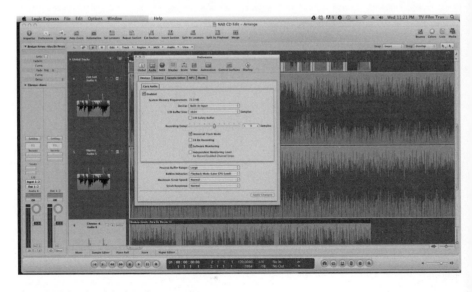

Figure 2.15 Logic global preference screen

MOTU (MARK OF THE UNICORN) DIGITAL PERFORMER

MOTU was at the forefront of technology in the mid '80s when they released Professional Composer and Performer for the Apple platform. Performer in particular took advantage of the newly formed technology of MIDI, otherwise known as Musical Instrument Digital Interface. Performer enabled the user to sequence numerous different instrument sounds through its extensive interface. To be fair, it was great if you were a keyboardist, yet *boring* if you were not. It is an interesting technology and has been convenient as it has grown through the years. But with the confusion of the many parameters and protocols, it can be frustrating for the average user. Today you can buy one plug-in to achieve what we previously had to use racks of sound modules and a plethora of MIDI cables for. Believe me, I used to have a MIDI studio.

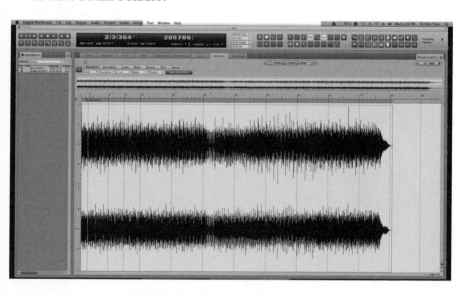

Figure 2.16 MOTU Digital Performer 8 waveform window

Figure 2.17 MOTU Digital Performer 8 tempo map window

Later in the '90s, MOTU came up with a way to sync audio and named the new software DP (Digital Performer), which was heads and tails better than Pro Tools but inferior when it came to editing and recording audio. However, the appeal of Digital Performer for some musicians was that the keyboard sounds ran virtually, while syncing to recorded audio live. This enabled the user to change keyboard sounds later after recording audio. It was great for people who were indecisive on committing to certain sound modules, letting them make last-minute changes during the mix. But with that being said, Digital Performer is still very popular among composers and keyboardists.

Figure 2.18 MOTU Digital Performer 8 volume map window

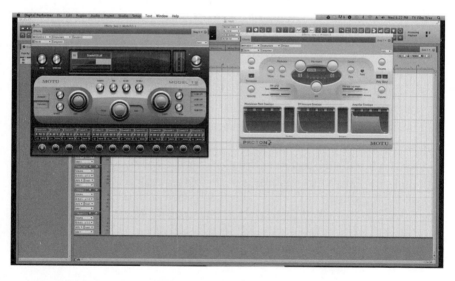

Figure 2.19 MOTU Digital Performer 8 multi plug-ins

Figure 2.20 MOTU Digital Performer 8 mixer

There are so many new music programs out there that it would take a whole book to list them and their attributes. Some others to look at are: Reason, Abelton Live, Cakewalk, Acid, Cubase, and Presonus Studio One (fig. 2.21). So this is where you have to think about what your application is going to be—editing, MIDI composing, recording live instruments, mastering, etc. All manufacturers offer trial downloads, so the best thing to do is try them out and see what system works best for your needs.

CHOOSING PLUG-INS

Figure 2.21 The World of Plug-Ins

Now that we are in a digital world, we have become accustomed to what is known as the VST, Virtual Studio Technology. Basically, this technology allows the integration between effects processing plug-ins like virtual synthesizers and recording platforms like Pro Tools and Logic. This was a large game-changer for audio recording, because you could use multi effects or dynamic processors for various tracks. For example, in the analog days, if you had one Urei 1176 limiter, you could only use it on one track or instrument. Now with UAD by Universal Audio, you can use the virtual 1176 plug-in on every track if so desired.

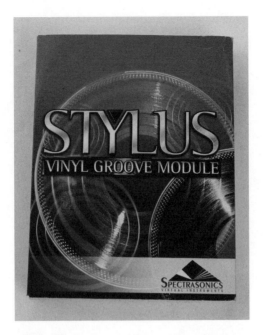

Figure 2.22 Spectrasonics Stylus RMX Virtual Groove plug-in

SPECTRASONICS

One of the most innovative and interesting plug-ins on the market today is the Spectrasonics Stylus RMX (fig. 2.22). I originally bought it back in the early 2000s before it was upgraded to RMX, and have used it on countless scores for television and film. Even today it is still a great tool and better than most of the other drum plug-ins on the market. The great thing about it is the extensive parameters, which allow you control of the grooves and tempo settings; plus, you can always expand your sound library with Propellerheads REX files. Spectrasonics incorporates what is called S.A.G.E. technology, Spectrasonics Advanced Groove Engine. If you are a composer, hip-hop producer, or a techno freak, this is the desert island virtual groove machine.

Figure 2.23 Spectrasonics Stylus RMX main screen page

Figure 2.24 Spectrasonics Stylus RMX effects screen

Figure 2.25 Spectrasonics Stylus RMX chaos editor

Figure 2.26 Spectrasonics Stylus RMX mixer

Spectrasonics offers an array of virtual instruments like their Legacy collection of Trilogy and Atmospheres, now replaced by their newer versions of Omnisphere and Trilian. This is the brainchild of chief sound designer of Roland keyboards, Eric Persing. But I think Stylus will be a mainstay for years to come with its flexibility and intuitiveness.

SLATE DIGITAL

Through the bombardment of overnight virtual instrument companies out there, it takes something special to crest over the crowd, and Steven Slate found it with his FG-X virtual mastering processor. The wonderful attribute of the FG-X: it boosts material to broadcast level without sonically squashing it, causing ear fatigue. So many of today's little magic plug-ins that claim to be the mastering tool secret change the inherent tone of the music, giving that overall shrill of EQ. Today you can hear it everywhere—hip hop, pop—that stupid loudness that brings a digital, cold, pasty-white feeling when you get to the verse. I found that FG-X was the most natural sounding and retains warmth to its gain boost. For the most part, I don't like to take on mastering. I believe my job as an artist, producer, and engineer is done when the mixes are finished. I am very happy to hand it over to a person who specializes in mastering; they have the correct equipment and the acoustical space to do the job. I'm not a big believer in the theory that one person sits in their space and tries to do everything. You need interaction with others to make good recordings; it is a group effort. Somewhere along the line, the twenty-first century attitude of someone doing the whole project—including writing, recording, producing, engineering, and mastering—became just a little too all-inclusive for me. Like the English poet John Donne wrote, "No man is an island, Entire of itself, Every man is a piece of the continent, A part of the main." With that being said, if you must master yourself, this is the best digital limiter that won't destroy your mix.

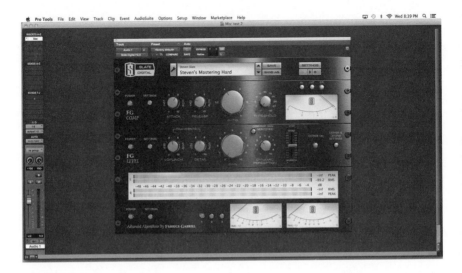

Figure 2.27 Slate FG-X mastering plug-in

Figure 2.28 Pro Tools BF-76 limiter like the Urei 1176

Slate Digital offers another interesting instrument called Trigger. Like its name, it is a trigger for drums, kick, snare, and toms. It works remarkably well and offers some great natural drum trigger sounds. This is probably the most useful plug-in ever made. I remember when we used to trigger drum sounds through an old Roland rack module and man, what a nightmare! The idea was to take the live drum sound of a snare or kick off of tape and put it through the sound module so that the original snare sound would trigger a new sound in one of the banks you choose on the module. You can only imagine what problems would arise. The fine-tuning on the threshold wasn't too accurate and any noisy snare would miss a trigger, causing all sorts of senseless sounds. It could take hours to get the trigger just right; it was like chasing after a ghost. Crazy daze for sure!

Figure 2.29 Slate Trigger original version

Figure 2.30 Slate Trigger 2 upgraded version

THE FRAY

There are many other plug-ins that can be used with standard programs like the UVI Workstation and Kontakt Player by Native Instruments. For instance, MOTU Symphonic Instruments and Tines Anthology both use the UVI Workstation to implement. The plug-in called First Call Horns uses Kontakt Player and is a very realistic horn software for its time. I used this program on some tracks when I produced the late great Randy Coven, bass extraordinaire. I had the idea that Randy needed something to interact with while playing his parts on his solo project entitled *Nu School*. The plug-in is based on actual live recorded horn section phrases and hits, so it sounded so much better than your typical run-of-the-mill Roland saxophone sounds.

Figure 2.31 Tines UVI Workstation realistic Rhodes sounds

Figure 2.32 Tines Bass UVI just like Ray Manzarek used with The Doors!

Figure 2.33 MOTU Symphonic Instruments UVI Workstation

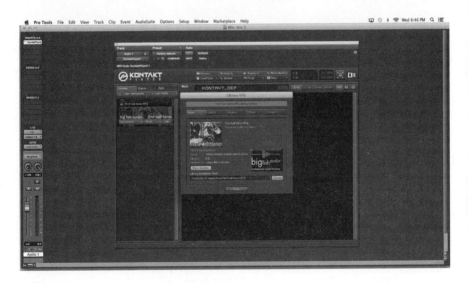

Figure 2.34 First Call Horns Kontakt Player

The company Discrete Drums has a compatible multi-track drum session on DVD for Pro Tools. The DVD is loaded with live drum performances, not just thiry-second loops, but eight- to sixteen-bar drum parts for verse, chorus, and middle eight as well as intros and endings. I have two of these discs, entitled *Heavy Mental Drums* and *EarthBeat,* and have had fantastic results (figs. 2.35 and 2.36). Each session uploads directly into Pro Tools and maps out each drum and percussion instrument, e.g., kick on track one, snare on track two, and so forth. This is an extremely useful tool, especially when composing for shows and album pre-production.

Figure 2.35 Discrete Drums EarthBeat Pro Tools Edition

Figure 2.37 Tines Anthology

Figure 2.36 Discrete Drums Heavy Mental Pro Tools Edition

Also worth mentioning is a company out of France called Arturia who makes some slick analog classic synth modeling plug-ins. Two of the most interesting ones are the Yamaha CS-80V and the Minimoog V (figs. 2.38 and 2.39). A lot of attention to detail was taken when recreating the actual interface of the keyboards. In fact, on the CS-80V it even has the fans moving just like the original beast. The actual sounds on both plug-ins are very well done and are very realistic to the originals. The only downside is that it takes quite a lot CPU to run, so to assure your computer doesn't become sluggish, record the sounds you decide on ASAP to an audio track.

Figure 2.38 Arturia Yamaha CS-80V Edition

Figure 2.39 Arturia Minimoog V Edition

Truly, there are so many plug-ins out on the market today, there is simply not enough time to go over all of them. As we discussed with DAW, manufacturers always offer free trials on software, which is the best way to test it before you buy it.

Figure 2.40 First Call Horns Edition

Figure 2.41 Dread Roots Reggae Edition

Figure 2.42 Epic Drums Edition

Figure 2.43 Metric Edition

SPEAKER MONITORS

This is a real important factor, so listen up! Remember, you will have to live day and night with your monitor choice. Even more importantly, you want monitors to give you a realistic perspective on how the rest of the world is going to hear your final mixes. Frank Zappa said in an interview once that he mixed on JBLs because a lot of his fans listen to JBLs on their home stereos. In the liner notes, he advised his listeners to place the EQ flat on the speakers. But it's all about ear fatigue and how you can avoid it with a decent set of monitors (fig. 2.44).

Figure 2.44 JBL 4410 studio monitor

Most mixing is done on near field monitors, and like with everything, it takes experience and knowledge to find the right pair. I recommend that you go down to your local pro audio store and bring music you are very familiar with on your iPod or phone and try it out on a few monitors. Though having said that, I would rather test monitors out with the full bandwidth wav files or even a CD as opposed to the MP3 versions. MP3s never sound very good and seem to lose a lot of the dynamic bandwidth. I never believed that there is an *all-in-one monitor* that could represent every consumer listening scenario. This is why I use three different monitors in the studio and check my mixes on each one to make sure everything is sitting just right. I use a classic pair of three-way JBL 4410s for large near fields, a pair of classic Yamaha NS-10s for a bookshelf reference (fig. 2.45), and a pair of Auratones strictly for television and radio mixes (fig. 2.46). I even have a mono button on the mixer to see if there is anything out of phase in the mixes.

Figure 2.45 The "Classic" Yamaha NS-10

Figure 2.46 The cube Auratone, an industry standard

Figure 2.47 Event Precision 8 monitor

I'm very old school and use a separate amplifier to power my monitors, but because everyone is in the box today the standard has become powered monitors. It always strikes me as funny at the AES (Audio Engineering Society) convention when all of these different monitor manufacturers carry on about the materials that are used to make their cones and voice coils, yet use a cheap amplification system in their speakers. Like with any other audio in your car or home, the speakers are only as good as the amplifier that powers them. Now you don't have to run and buy the most expensive pair of monitors thinking you will have great mixes in an instant, that's just not the case. Further, you don't need very expensive monitors to get great mixes either. Remember, the Yamaha NS-10s were very cheap and they were used in every studio around the world for years. Countless classic records were mixed on NS-10s, so the price tag doesn't mean anything! So there is a happy medium between buying monitors. Best way is to use your ears!

Today there are so many powered monitors to choose from in all price ranges it boggles the mind. So when choosing, keep in mind your room size, how close you'll be when mixing, your recording setup, and of course the style of music you will most often be recording. Some brands to look at are JBL, Yamaha, Event, Neumann, Dynaudio, and Genelec. I remember years ago I had a pair of bookshelf Tannoys and they never sounded good, no matter what room I put them in to mix. All of the mid-range seemed to be scooped out with a spoon, and all I got was lows and highs. Needless to say, I sold those real fast. I used to run out to the car to check my mixes. But that became so tedious and so many factors could change with the car sound system. This is why I settled on having three different pairs of monitors in the studio, to make sure the mixes would sound good in all forums.

ISOLATION BOOTH

It is what it is! This is a simple booth with a door to isolate the sound within, whether it is a vocal over dub, a guitar amp, or an actual drummer. Being a guitarist with a large collection of tube amps, I find this to be an integral part of my studio. Where in heaven's name would I put all of the Marshalls, Fenders, Orange amps, etc.? Naturally, in an iso booth so I can record at ridiculously high volumes. Right? You see, I was thrown out of a few apartments in Los Angeles years ago because of sheer volume, or "disturbing the peace" as they called it, I forget now. Even growing up in my parent's high-rise apartment in NYC, the city that never sleeps, the complaints from the other tenants poured in because of my outrageous tonal qualities on the guitar—loud, perhaps, yet essential. That sweet tone that vibrates through the amp can only be achieved at deafening decibels. That's why man came out with the ever-clever Master Volume knob, though between us, it's just not the same, but that's for a different chapter.

Figure 2.48 Isolation booth filled with deafening demons!

Figure 2.49 Isolation booth miked up for high decibels!

Figure 2.50 Marshall Amp close miked with Sure 57 inside isolation booth

My particular booth is four by four by eight feet and is just right for my needs. However, you can buy them in all configurations, with windows and even a ventilation fan so your singer won't faint from lack of oxygen. Some of the manufacturers today have guitar amplifier iso booths specifically designed to fit a combo amp or half stack Marshall. Check out VocalBooth.com, Whisper Room, Clear Sonic, Studio Box, and GK Sound Booths for more ideas.

Chapter 3
Engineering vs. Producing

Figure 3.1 Brian Tarquin in the studio with Trident recording console

Engineering and producing really go hand and hand. This is why so many great producers started out as engineers, and some of the best were musicians: case in point, Roy Thomas Baker, Frank Zappa, Quincy Jones, and Bob Rock. Basically, an engineer handles the technical part of the session, ensuring everything is in phase, clean recordings, correct positioning of the microphones, and hands on for all recording procedures, like playback, recording, etc. Now the producer is the one who is the real liaison to the band or artist. He makes sure the band's and his vision is reached during the sessions.

The producer will usually explain what he wants to hear from the engineer, like a fat snare or a jangly guitar tone, and then the engineer will make it happen in the recording process. The producer is also responsible for the overall budget of the recording, including hiring outside musicians and overseeing that the session flows smoothly by taking some of the pressure off of the artist so he or she can concentrate on the performance. Experienced producers can make the difference in the artist's performance by motivating them to give their best in show. This is extremely important, because I've been in sessions where the artist's trust in the producer was lost and the session completely fell apart. So the bond between artist and producer has to be strong and there has to be trust on both sides to get great recordings.

After twenty-five years, I can tell right away what's going to work and what's not. I remember engineering and producing the late great bass player Randy Coven for his album *Nu School*. He was such a fantastic talent, but in the studio he had to be controlled and guided through the process in order to get a good performance. In his previous albums I felt he was always overshadowed by the guitarist, so on this release I wanted him to be the center of attention; after all it was *his* solo record. He always wanted me to play guitar on the songs and I did on a couple, but I always said, "Forget about guitar. Let's get a keyboardist instead, so you can shine!" On his insistence we went through so many guitarists it was like a necropolis, but finally in the end, he understood what I was going for and we used a keyboardist. Doing so, you could really hear the bass nuances that would have been lost with hard rock guitars. He loved the end result, and I believe the recording possessed the top bass performances of his career. I pushed him to experiment and had him play on these funky grooves I programmed on Stylus RMX with horn hits, and they turned into the songs featured on *Nu School* and *Urban Suburban*. He killed it, playing some fantastic solos *à la* Jaco Pastorius.

Figure 3.2 Randy Coven recording *Nu School* at Jungle Room Studios

I don't care what anyone says, if you can't play your instrument, you have no business being in the studio. I'm not going to sit in front of a screen for hours cutting and pasting performances together because musicians can't play the goddamn song correctly! Practice and come back when you know it! In the past, I've told bands and artists that you better be well rehearsed, because school is out and you should have it all together when we start recording. Those people out there who say playing is not everything obviously can't play. You're a musician, right? Then learn how to play your instrument. So many composers I've known couldn't play a three-minute song if their life depended on it. Why? Because they are so used to this MIDI, virtual instrument crap that requires little or no brainpower that they become lazy, just copying and pasting two-bar phrases all over the place to make up some cue. This is the world we live in today; it's the instant gratification generation because of the Internet. I remember growing up in New York City, sitting in my parent's apartment practicing guitar day after day, gradually getting better and seeing a great improvement through the years, which came with a real gratification. Just like the bands I was in, practicing until we got the music right and playing out live to get better. You shouldn't do it if you don't love playing your instrument!

Now, of course, having said that, sometimes you may have to bend the rules for *bona fide* rock stars. Case in point: when I was recording Leslie West. Randy had brought him in to play on a couple of songs for the album, and of course West was not prepared and had not even heard the songs. At least he knew what he wanted for tone. I had an old Marshall JCM 800 in the studio with a Marshall cabinet, so he plugged into my Ibanez Tube Screamer and turned all knobs on the amp to ten and we started recording. With that, the orders came bellowing out of West's mouth: turn me up, turn him down, more delay, less drums, get me a diet Coke, and where the hell is Coven? Of course Randy was so nervous he was outside smoking a pack of cigarettes. But that is just how some sessions go. Keep in mind I was recording Leslie on an Ampex MM1200 twenty-four-track two-inch tape machine and he was constantly impatient about the tape rolling back to the punch-in point. Finally I said to him, "Dude, didn't you record all of those Mountain records on analog tape? Most of you probably don't realize that each analog machine had its own idiosyncrasies and the Ampex MM 1200 had a delay in punch-in, so it always sounded as if you cut off the first note of the punch, but it was fine when you listened to playback." So he was freaking out about that too, thinking I cut the first note off, but he calmed down when he heard it played back. All this plays with your mind in the studio as an engineer, so you have to keep your cool, because in this case, you may be the only calm one in the room! After the Leslie West session I had to dump the tapes to Pro Tools and do all sorts of edits to his guitar parts, copy and paste hell. But in the end it all worked out and Randy was very happy with the outcome.

Figure 3.3 Randy Coven, Leslie West, and Brian Tarquin cutting tracks at Jungle Room Studios

The biggest advice I can give a band going into a recording session is to do it all at the same time. In other words, don't record each instrument separately. If it is a three-piece band, then get everyone in the room and record, using some isolation with baffles on the drums. I can't stress how important it is to have that energy with all of the musicians in the same room. When I was recording the basic tracks (drums, bass, rhythm guitars) for my last project, *Guitars for Wounded Warriors*, I engineered, produced, and played guitar at the same time onto the Ampex MM 1200. I even had an assistant operating the tape machine and reading numbers. You really have to be on your game for this; it's not like you just hit the space bar or whatever, there is no "undo" button for tape! If you record over something or erase another track by accident because you had the wrong track armed, you *screwed the pooch*! I've been there and it's not fun to have to explain to people why their parts have been reduced again because you screwed up. But you really become a part of the music, constantly watching the meters on the compressors, recording levels on the tape machine, moving faders and adjusting effects levels.

Figure 3.4 Brian Tarquin Guitar & Engineering plus Rick Mullen Bass in *Guitars for Wounded Warriors* sessions
Photograph by Miss M

There is huge advantage today with the digital age because you don't have to worry about all of the little tactile things any longer; it's really plug and play. The great advantage I can say about Pro Tools is that you are able to easily fly in tracks, which was completely unheard of in the analog days. I do this quite a lot with artists around the world; I will have a track all done and want a solo by Steve Morse, Hal Lindes, Gary Hoey, or Billy Sheehan and even if they are on tour, they can do it on their DAW and Dropbox me the files, which I easily import into my sessions. *Voilà*, you have them right in the studio with you. However, I do prefer to have the artist playing with me in the studio to get the vibe, so I can communicate with them on direction and feel. But putting all digital vs. analog aside, the only way you get the tones and sounds is to *use your ears!* Don't let the computer do the work for you—use it as a tool, like any other studio piece of gear. I found the best tools are using both digital and analog together, like a DAW running audio through an analog console so you're not stuck in the box and you get the best of both worlds. You have the ease of the waveform editing, along with using each channel of the analog mixer for EQs, effects, and outboard gear. Perfect marriage!

The following are interviews from some of the greatest engineers and producers I've personally known. They talk about how they got into the business and their favorite tools, instruments, and tricks of the trade. So don't just take my advice—listen to these guys, too!

NEIL DORFSMAN *INTERVIEW*

Figure 3.5 Neil Dorfsman chilling in the studio in front of the Neve

Grammy-winning engineer/producer Neil Dorfsman, has had an illustrious career recording famous artists such as Paul McCartney, Bruce Springsteen, Dire Straits, Sting, Bob Dylan, The Rolling Stones, Billy Idol, and the list goes on. He is a wonderful, soft-spoken guy who possesses the extraordinary talent of keeping sessions moving forward and getting the right performances from artists. From his struggling beginnings in the early '70s to being Eddie Kramer's assistant in recording Kiss albums at Electric Lady Studios, and then becoming the first engineer at the Power Station, he has a lot of advice to give, so be ready to listen up!

Give us a little background on how you got started in studio recording, becoming entranced with engineering.

I knew early on in life that I somehow wanted to make records. I always had a huge record collection and always listened to records. I listened from a slightly different point of view of how they got things and why they did things and how they got the sounds they did. I went out to Los Angeles after college trying to get a job in the studio business. I had an interview at The Beach Boys' studio and the first question they asked me was what my astrological sign was and I didn't know it, so the interview ended right there. I spent a little more time in L.A., but came back to New York in the mid '70s and got a job recording voice-overs for commercials. It was just a two-track studio with a stock library, but soon I became frustrated with it.

I sent out about 100 resumes to studios on the east coast and got a call back from Electric Lady Studios in 1978. I became Eddie Kramer's assistant, who, as you know, recorded Jimi Hendrix, Led Zeppelin, and a bunch of other legendary bands. The first record I worked with him on was Kiss's *Alive II* and also *Love Gun*, in which he trained me. We then were mixing the album *Stone Blue* together at the Power Station for the band Foghat. After the album was done, Power Station wound up hiring me late in '79. The record I got to engineer on my own as head engineer was Bruce Springsteen's *The River*. So I started at the Power Station as an assistant, but quickly became an engineer.

How do you balance producing and engineering in the studio? Give some key elements on keeping a session intact when dealing with artists.

I've always been into music, but I don't play. So I thought being a producer/engineer was a way of being surrounded by it without being a musician. Plus, I enjoy the artistic things that producing and engineering required. As far as balancing them in the studio, I always try to engineer the records I produce even though it is very difficult to split those tasks. It is two different parts of your brain and pretty difficult to concentrate on performances, the vibe, as well as the technical end of things.

When I'm making a record I use the engineering to create the energy I want in the production and I try to get the sounds as close to the final sounds as possible. So, in other words, I don't wait until the end mix to get the final sounds. To me, making music is really about balancing energy. It's a constant back and forth process between the producing and engineering. As far as the artists go, I've been so lucky to work with some amazing, incredible artists, from Bruce Springsteen and Paul McCartney to Dire Straits, Bob Dylan, Bruce Hornsby, and many, many others. When you are doing a session, it is very important to work fast, and with my background in assisting, doing voice-overs and commercial jingles, it taught me to work fast. Working quickly is key to keeping the artists inspired. So I try not to let the engineering get in the way if I can help it. I'm always trying to get into the artists' frame of mind and vision, but also give them enough space to create that vision on their own.

Someone once told me early on in my career that as a producer they weren't willing to work with an artist that they weren't willing to lose an argument to, which is really good advice. An artist needs to have a vision; you can't impose it on them. As George Martin said, you can drive the bus, but you need the passengers (the band) to tell you where they want to go. I learned slowly over the years that production has a psychological component to it as well as a technical, musical component. When a session is good, all of those components are working well and the band trusts you and understands what you need from them. There is a creative give and take. You challenge them in some ways and they hopefully rise to the challenge or present something new to you.

What is your trick on miking drums when recording?

There is no real trick to miking drums. I tend to multi mic more than most people to try and get as much information during a live performance as possible, and try and weed through it a little bit and decide what I'm going to use. I don't tend to wind up with tons of microphones but I do set them up and make decisions fairly quickly on what I like and what I am going to use. I try to capture as much sonic energy that is passing through the room in a brief window of time as possible. I'm trying to grab and preserve as many "angles" as possible to the sound coming off the floor.

Figure 3.6 Neil Dorfsman drum miking techniques with multiple microphones

CHIMENE BADI SESSION DRUM SET-UP

STUDIO	INPUT	MIC & NOTES	TREATMENT
6	KICK 1	NEIL'S BEYER 88 OR 52 (INSIDE)	MEQ
7	KICK 1	FET 47 –10DB (OUTSIDE)	MASSENBERG 8200
8	KICK 1	PZM (OUTSIDE)	
9	KICK 1	YAMAHA SUBKICK	
11	XTRA KICK	EV 868	MEQ
12	XTRA KICK	EV M88	MASSENBERG 8200
14	SNARE 1	SHURE 56 (TOP)	EQP

15	SNARE 1	SM 57 (BTM)	GATE
16	SNARE 1	NEIL'S EM101 (RIM)	
17	SNARE 2	SHURE 56 (top)	EQP
18	SNARE 2	SM 57 (btm)	GATE
19	TOM 1	421 (Top)	EQP
20	TOM 1	421 (BTM)	GATE
21-26	TOM 2-4	421 (top/BTM)	EQP / GATES
27	HIHAT	451- 20DB WITH "BENDER"	
28	CYM (DRUMMERS' L)	460 –20	
29	CYM (DRUMMERS' C)	460 –20	
30	CYM (DRUMMERS' R)	460 –20	
31	MONO AMB	NEIL'S BRAUNER VMA	DISTRESSOR
32/33	CLOSE AMBIENCE	COLES L/R	SMART COMPRESSOR
34/35	FAR AMBIENCE	AVATAR APEX MICS L/R	LA3A
36	BACK AMBIENCE	RCA 44	1176
37	LOOP MIC UNDER SNARE	NEIL'S BULLET MIC	

Snare

On the top of the snare I use a Shure Beta 56, and the bottom a Shure SM57. I didn't used to record the bottom of the snare, but producers seem to like a more "snare-y" snare drum now. I have a little Country-man EM101 microphone, which I used to tape to the rim of the snare to open a gate on the top and bottom mic if the guy was playing really loud. Recently I started recording it, and it gives you a metallic, ring-y sound. It injects some personality into the drum.

Toms

I use Sennheiser 421s to mic toms on the top and the bottom. I gate the bottom mics on the drums, and I flip the phase relative to the top. I have the gates set to open even if the drummer taps pretty slightly. The bottom mic provides something fundamental to the tone of the drum.

Figure 3.7 Neil Dorfsman front view drum miking techniques

Kick

I use a Shure 52 Beta or a Beyer M88 inside the kick. I use a Neumann 47 FET outside and in front of the kick, about seven inches from the front of the head. I'll put the head of the mic three or four inches inside the front hole. I try to feel where the air pressure is ending, and put the mic at that point where the wave seems to end. I put it at an angle towards the rim to the corner circumference of the drum shell. I'm finding I get a little more tone that way. That mic is low down in the drum physically, below the equator of the drum, pointing slightly to the side.

Overheads

I use AKG 460s as overheads, one to the left of the bass drum, and one to the right. I measure their distance from the top of the kick drum, and point them straight down at the cymbals, as I'm trying to get a clean recording of the cymbals and snare drum. For the ambient mics I use two Coles 4038 mics eight feet in front of the drums, about waist high. I put little gobos around them to cut down on the room size, then hammered them pretty hard with an SSL "SMART" compressor.

I also have my own Brauner VMA, a super high-end microphone that I put in front of the drums ten feet away, in omni, about chest high. I squashed it with an Empirical Labs Distressor, going for a modified hi-fi sound. It's pretty compressed, but an accurate representation of what's going on in the room. I change the Brauner from cardioid to omni depending on how much life the producer wanted on the kit. I varied the attack and release on the compression, and I would compress it hard, about ten decibels.

What advice can you give the novice home engineers on getting good sounding tracks?

I would say you are using two sides of your brain, the technical part and the creative part. I would caution to not get overly technical with everything, and to use your ears. Another person early in my career said everybody listens, but not everybody hears. I thought that was a wise thing to say because you really have to listen and not get carried away with the technical ends of things. Also today it's so easy to get carried away with plug-ins and bundles. They put these together by famous mixers, who are brilliant, but the plug-ins will only get you so far. Presets are meant to be a starting-off point. The thing to do is to start with them and make them your own as much as possible.

You can't underestimate good-sounding equipment, a good microphone, at least one good condenser microphone, a good-sounding pre-amp—I love Neve's—maybe a good compressor, a good EQ—that's really important! There are great inexpensive microphones like 57s and such that are key. It's very important to find the microphones that you like and that work for you, and to have your own go-to toolbox. For example, microphones that work for guitars are a 57 and a Royer 121, or an AKG 451 and a Sennheiser 421, or whatever pleases you. For vocals, have a good quality condenser and a good quality dynamic like a SM7 or even a 58. Getting good tracks is really a function of not only having a decent player with good equipment on his end, but also having some decent equipment of your own, like a microphone, compressor, EQ, that kind of thing. Also really listening is a factor. When someone is playing, listen to the context of the song, don't isolate things too much; everything has to relate to everything else.

You can use the engineering as a tool with the production to make sure the sounds are working together and advancing the overall vibe of the tune. I would also add that it is really important to approach the work we do as producers and engineers and musicians with humility and a bit of gratitude. It's a very demanding and difficult job, but I know when we are doing it we feel incredibly lucky. I've been in some situations in the studio where they have been virtually life changing, so moving and spiritual in a way. I've learned through the years making many mistakes how important it is to project generosity and open-mindedness, and my bedside manner has improved. I think that is very important because it is supposed to be on some level fun and at the same time it is extremely difficult and stressful. So you have to keep all of these elements in perspective.

Mixing is always the issue for home recording engineers because of the limitations of their DAW. What advice can you give to those who mix in the box?

I don't really relate to the physicality of it. I like the tactile process of working on a large format analog console and am able to do multiple things at one time and actually turn knobs. Somehow I feel I can get a closer connection to what's going on that way. I don't enjoy staring at a screen and find that I get overly technical when I'm mixing that way.

Something to keep in mind is you can get a pretty good mix in the first three to four hours and have it 90 percent there, but what really separates an excellent mix from an okay one is that last 10 percent. This is the last several hours of work, the minute details, sort of getting underneath the hood and getting to the details of the mix. The little things like the rides, the effects, and stuff that bring a mix to life. So I would say let the plug-ins take you a certain distance, but always have a vision in your mind of where you want to get to and don't think because the plug-in says vocal or snare drum that's all you gotta do. Add your own elements and personality, that's what mixing is all about. When you are the mixer you become the artist, the band is supplying you with the raw material, so to speak, and you need to have an artistic vision when you are mixing. It's just not a matter of balancing, it's a matter of creating a landscape or a movie scene or several movie scenes.

It's funny, one of my students said to me that mixing on my Trident console was so much easier and intuitive than mixing on his laptop with a mouse, the only way he has ever known. Do you find that the new generation has become too reliant on computers to do the work for them when it comes to recording and mixing?

I do find mixing on an analog board a lot more intuitive and easier than mixing on a laptop or a mouse. Even though I have a D Command in my home studio, which has faders, it still somehow feels like a giant mouse, which it is. I don't think the new generation has become too reliant on computers to do the work for them, but I don't think they have had the experience of knowing what the other side of things is.

They are constantly calling analog gear "old school"—it's a weird term to use for real gear. There are some great ones out there; I just never want to A/B the plug-in to the original. In some cases, they might be the same, but in many cases they're not. And there is really nothing you can do about that because most people won't get to work in a large format analog room with a big selection of outboard gear.

GEOFF GRAY OF FAR & AWAY STUDIOS
INTERVIEW

Figure 3.8 Geoff Gray making the music behind his Sony mixer

My dear friend and engineer mentor Geoff Gray now resides in Boulder, Colorado, with his studio Far & Away Studios. But when we first met over twenty years ago, his studio was in the small hamlet of Goshen, New York, housed in a 200-year-old barn. I soon became his assistant engineer after our first encounter and the wonderful musical journey began. I can still smell the cigarette smoke, the stale beer bottles in the corner, and the musical testosterone in the air. Yes, there is nothing like the smell of musicianship in the studio mixed with electrical solder melting and the fresh stench of a new reel of analog tape permeating the senses.

It is important to note that back then there was no "undo" feature, no computer recording, and certainly no cut and paste. Yes, that's right! Men were men and we had to physically splice tape to edit with a trusty rusty razor, old sticky splicing tape and a stogie hanging out of our mouth. In fact, the newest technology then was DAT recorders, digital-audio-tape, which utilized a small tape cartridge to record music digitally. Believe me, that was a big deal because it did away with the quarter-inch and half-inch tape masters; that is, until we realized many years later tape did sound better!

Well, maybe it was the smoke, the alcohol, the drugs, or the combination of them all that made the mixes sound better. I don't know, but I always laugh when I see audio gear for sale today on eBay stating proudly by the owner it was used in a "smoke-free" studio. Does that make a bit of difference? I own old Urei compressors from smoke-filled studios that sound better than the most strenuously *antiseptic*, antifungal compressors wrapped in baby wipes. I think we need a little putrid, foul bacteria to reek up our favorite controls and knobs. It gives that lived-in feel, sending a message to people that you really used your equipment and broke it in properly, not to mention adding that certain *je ne sais quoi* to the mix. But seriously don't get too hung up on the overall condition of something, just how it sounds! Geoff has some great advice on getting your home recordings to sound better, so listen up.

Give us a little background on how you got started in studio recording, becoming entranced with engineering.

I was lucky to have 914 Studios near my hometown. 914 was always busy with some major project like Blood, Sweat, and Tears, Dusty Springfield, or Janis Ian who received album of the year for *Between the Lines* with my future production partner, David Snider, on guitar.

The timing was right for me to walk in the control room for the very first time and see a friend from high school named Larry Alexander behind the board. It wasn't long before Larry was recording my band's first vinyl release. At one point in a mix with my band, Larry asked if I could push up a couple of faders while he was tied up doing something else in that part of the song. I was terrified and thrilled at the same time. I didn't mess it up. By the time Larry did the fade I had made up my mind that this is where I belonged . . . on the console side of the window. Larry eventually became a staff engineer at Power Station in New York and once again I was privy to amazing gear, acoustics, studio design, and engineering tricks.

The smell of 3M tape was more addicting than anything I've ever encountered. That first night, engineer Louis Lahav was working on some commercials. I got to watch a friend put down some guitar tracks. I fell in love with the process of recording. Louis was working with some guy named Bruce Springsteen during the day on some *Born to Run* record. Eric Weissberg and the band Deliverance had just finished up some mixes on *Rural Free Delivery*. The excitement on these older dudes' faces was intoxicating. I'll have what they're having. Pre Dropbox! I remember Steve Mandel exuberantly holding the phone up to a playback speaker to someone in Nashville just beaming. When the record came out I was so excited to have that feeling of being near the talent and the process.

The man for me to thank is Brooks Arthur, who was an owner of 914. He graciously let his engineers work late nights on their own spec projects. It's here I got to sit in on a lot of wonderful studio moments. Danny Toan's album *First Serve* landed a deal with Atlantic Records. I got to be there for some of that project. For me, there's nothing better than listening to a commercial release and remembering the moments I experienced in the studio that contributed to how the final product sounds. Ironically, at the same time in my life I got to meet Les Paul. We would become lifetime friends. Talk about having a friend in the business! I'm pretty sure none of us would be reading this if it weren't for Les' inventions. I bought my first Ampex AG 350 four-track from Les. A second irony is that my machine originally came from Mira Sound where Brooks had worked eight or so years before. He set me on the right track to buy only the best gear I could find.

So when the opportunity arose to start Far & Away Studios, Inc. with partner Rick Greenwald on a great piece of real estate that fit our requirements perfectly, I was so there and jumped at the chance.

You had a great space when we first met, many moons ago, in a two-hundred-year-old New York barn. How did you decide on what gear to buy at first and why?

The space was great and it was to due to the room being treated in wood, four-inch, six-inch, and eight-inch widths in a repeating pattern. That room was constructed in 1943, but Tony Bongiovi used a similar distribution of wood when he and Bob Walters built Power Station.

Gear selection had to be dictated by budget in those early years. Everything we made we put back into the business. Sometimes we had to wait a little longer to buy what was a better piece. The landscape is so much better now for the home recordist. Great vintage gear is still around, but plug-ins get the job done. My experience is that plug-ins don't really sound the same as the originals but they sound very good and can be more useful in some instances because you're not limited by the original's number of channels.

Sometimes in the early learning curve you have to use what you've got. We got great direction in our first condenser mic purchase, the venerable AKG 414 with a C12 capsule. It was shockingly accurate. I had to do a jazz date and only had three mics I could use on drums. I had a kick mic, a '57 to share snare and hat, and put the 414 in bidirectional mode, placed it with the lobes facing the cymbals. I hoped it would pick up toms. It worked great. The drummer was flipping out about the sound. Sort of a Glyn Johns technique before I knew what that was. It was because we had the restriction on the number of mics. The takeaway is that the phase interference from too many drums mics can really muck up the sound. I always think of that when approaching a kit.

To get back to the question, the more money that came in the more good mics and outboard we could buy and that's the endless loop of studio ownership.

Figure 3.9 Geoff Gray at Far & Away Studios. Whoever has the most gear wins!

I remember us recording late-night sessions and smelling the half-inch analog tape wearing away with each passing recording. What recording platform do you use today?

We are in a great age right now where we can meld analog and digital for the strengths of each medium: tape and DAW, analog outboard, and plug-ins. We appreciate our DAW for all the amazing things that we can do with it.

I really miss the sound of tape for drums and bass. I miss it for other things, too, but mostly the impact of percussive hits. Tape has a depth that you can discern as front-to-back dimension in the monitors and a punch that sets it apart. Remember that tape compression is happening on every track if you are keeping your levels where they should be. It's actually like having a compressor on every track, so the final outcome is really fat, hot mixes.

When tracking we have a two-inch Studer tape machine running that is "normal-ed" in our patch bay directly to Pro Tools analog in. We have designed a template that can offset the time differences and instantly line up the digital and analog tracks perfectly. No wasting time transferring from tape to digital. We use an old Teletronix LA 2A tube compressor for most of the overdubs and an abundance of tube microphones to keep warm signals going to the DAW after the tracking process. During mix down we're fortunate to have a Fairchild 670 kissing the mix bus and going to a half-inch Studer tape machine running at fifteen IPS with a CCIR alignment. CCIR is the European standard versus NAB, the American standard. Good enough for The Beatles, good enough for us!

What is your trick on miking drums when recording?

Well, I guess they are tricks but I think I see them as best choices due to experience. The first axiom is kick, snare, and toms go to tape. I like the cymbals going to digital. This also helps keep sonic separation in the mix. An EV RE 20 is our go-to inside kick mic. It's about two inches from the beater at about a forty-five-degree angle so the plosives go past it. This goes to a Neve pre and Lindell compressor set to a slow attack and fast release. This is a huge "trick." The slow setting on the compressor lets the attack get by without affecting the transients. The quick release makes it wickedly percussive. This works well on popping bass too.

Next is an old Shure SM 57 on the snare going to a Neve pre. I've been using a Sennheiser 441 on the snare bottom with nice results. The toms are miked with Sennheiser 421s going into Grace preamps. They are glorious and manufactured up the road from us. I think I depart from some engineers on overheads. I hate other drums in the overheads. They're cymbal mics to me. I like to roll off the bottom on two more Neve pres for these mics. We have a Ramsa mini condenser mic for the hi-hat. We got it on a trial evaluation, then we were told to keep it. If it ever dies, I'm screwed.

I have a Crown PZM mic going through an API 512 pre for the kick and it's sitting on the quilt. I add 46 Hz in the mix to that. Two more Crown PZMs are on the back wall doing beautiful things to cymbals. They are pre-amped by two API 312 cards. On the hi-hat is an API 312 as well. We have two stellar-sounding DPA mics hanging in front of and above the kit. They go through a Symetrix 202 mic pre. It's one of my all-time favorite pres. The two Coles 4038s go through more Grace pres set in the ribbon mode. This makes a colossal difference in ribbon performance. The Coles are back about ten feet from the kit and up about twelve feet in the air.

After my talk about minimalist drum miking, please take into account that we are not using all these mics all the time. Many folks track here and I export the files to them. They can pick and choose. One of my "tricks" I learned from Larry at Power Station, now Avatar Studios, is true gated reverb. The concept is to take an analog snare output from Pro Tools to the trigger input on a two-channel noise gate (big love for our Drawmer 201s). This gate has the room mics running through both channels. When the snare hits, it opens the room mics for just an instant and introduces that big snare room sound to the mix.

We always prepare a day in advance of a session involving drums. There are a lot of mics and pres and if it can go wrong . . . we check the signal path for every mic and walk into the date feeling reasonably sure we've done all we can to not let the client down.

What advice can you give the novice home engineers on getting good-sounding tracks?

The first thing I would suggest is to get an optimized signal path. By that I mean the pre-amp level in the perfect sweet spot, the compressor staying in check, and the board/DAW levels ideal. This is not that easy. In the case of a singer, have them sing the loudest passage in the song. You need to explain that this has to be done a few times so that you, as engineer, are doing right by the singer. Explain that this is ultimately for their benefit and to get the best sound possible. It's time to get political. Take charge and make the person absolutely know that you are doing this on their behalf.

There's nothing worse than sitting there watching a great take go down with the pre-amp overdriving, the compressor barely moving (not that you are always using a compressor), and a tiny waveform on the screen. I really like tracking with an LA 2A compressor on vocals, as it adds a nice presence and is very gentle in its response. I tell all my students not to track with a compressor that has more than two knobs. There's no undo. If all the gear in the signal path is running in the correct operating range, you've done a good thing for the client and for your reputation. Any good producer will allot you the time to "borrow" the talent for these level checks.

One last thing: bring all these levels down a touch once you find them. A singer will always sing louder during a real take. (Drummers every time!) When all is optimized, you can love the fact that you can edit between a batch of takes and they will match. Had you changed things through all the takes, they may not have the same sound and you'll be gaining things up and down to get them to match.

Another political message to the band: "I cannot get you perfect levels in the cans until I get perfect levels going through the gear and to the DAW." It's unfortunate that this crucial step is the last step, but that's the way it is. You work from the inside out.

Mixing is always the issue for home recording engineers because of the limitations of their DAW. What advice can you give to those who mix in the box?

Get out now! Just kidding. There have been many fine in-the-box mixes, but for me, nothing compares to sitting behind a console with a hand full of faders and playing the board like an instrument. When I'm working with a producer, it's often a four-handed affair. I liken live mixes to a whole band recording at the same time in our big room. There is an energy that evolves from the forced concentration and knowing that this is in real time. The heart rate certainly goes up. See if you can get an invite to a professional studio that has a console and see the difference. Once a mix is really close to perfect, we turn on the automation and commit to it. After that initial rush, we go back and ride individual faders to perfect the mix.

Also, all that I said about maintaining proper levels through the signal chain applies in the box even more so. Professional analog outboard has a lot of headroom and if pushed, may also give a desirable effect. Not so much with cartoons (plug-ins). I find having a monitor in front of me is an acoustic drawback. Reflections can really mess with your stereo imaging. If you're tracking bands at home, try to lay the room out so that you are facing the artist(s). I get a stiff neck in studios with the artists to the left or right, and having the talent behind you just doesn't make sense. I get so many cues as to the quality of the performance from looking at the talent. One grimace from the talent and my assistant, Alex Stricker, is writing down the measure number. Like Les Paul, we don't have a control room window and are in the same room as the artist. Listening to performances through headphones can be very revealing; no one is telling the latest drummer jokes and the artist feels that you're more intimately involved.

It's funny, one of my students said to me that mixing on my Trident console was so much easier and intuitive than mixing on his laptop with a mouse, the only way he has ever known. Do you find that the new generation has become too reliant on computers to do the work for them when it comes to recording and mixing?

I would just like to make sure the newer generation can experience where all this came from and to listen to tape vs. digital. I've heard the great engineer, Bruce Swedien, play a mind-blowing recording that he did in 1955 on a three-track Ampex. I'm still chasing that quality. It really turned my head around to hear that.

Working on an automated large format console is a tactile experience and also quicker. I find being in the box too isolating. I prefer hands-on, not finger-on. A small controller is just as debilitating.

To answer the second part, yes. It's cool to have unlimited takes to comp together, but it's so easy to punch in fixes on the spot. I'd rather have a really good punched take to work with and keep the backup takes to edit from. I find it quicker and better than a pile of sort of okay takes that mean hours of work to get one perfect performance after the fact. For vocal performances, I try not to rely on auto tune. Auto tune sounds more realistic if it isn't pushed hard, so I'll work to get it correct in the first place. I've trained myself to go back to listening, not staring at a screen. I love being able to edit on a DAW and I'm okay with recording on one.

PAUL OROFINO *INTERVIEW*

In the New York's Hudson Valley there is a wealth of musical talent and interesting, cool, hideaway recording studios, one of them being Paul Orofino's, Millbrook Sound Studios. The studio's credits include engineering and producing Blue Öyster Cult, Leslie West & Mountain, Randy Coven, The Cars, and Foghat. Through the many changes in the music recording industry, Paul has redesigned his studio to be a more intimate space, calling it The House of Music and offering musicians an array of vintage gear. It's great to see engineers still using classic analog gear and Paul has quite a collection, plus he has the Otari Radar II (Hard Disc Recorder) twenty-four-track twenty-four-bit, probably one of the best digital recorders made because of its converters; beats any DAW system out there today. Paul shares his experience in the studio with us, so make sure you take notes!

Give us a little background on how you got started in studio recording.

Let's see, when I was around fifteen, sixteen years old, around 1972, I started playing in cover bands in my neighborhood (Queens, New York). At the time, there were many bars, clubs, halls, school dances, and churches that had music on a weekly basis and they all needed live bands . . . as the DJ thing hadn't happened as yet.

Now to get the band ready to perform all these gigs, we needed a place to rehearse, and rehearse quite a few times a week. We tried all of our mom and dad's basements and garages, but trust me this got old pretty quick. Especially in my case as I lived in a row of attached houses in Queens, needless to say the neighbors didn't take too kindly to us rehearsing as often as we wanted to. That being said, I decided I had to find a better way. So I searched every day after school for a storefront, a basement of a store, back of a warehouse, basically any place from anyone that would rent to me (remember, I was just a teenager). I needed a space to rent for a year or more that we could make noise in without disturbing anyone around. It took a few months, but I found one . . . it was the basement of a record store (Moonshine Records) in Bay Terrace, Queens, and they agreed to a long-term lease with me. The owners were very cool music guys and at the time probably about ten years older then I, but they were open to a long-term lease, and liked the idea of a band rehearsing downstairs. The only thing they asked of me was if we could not start till they were closed each night, about 5 PM, and that was fine with us, so we were in.

Okay, fast forward a few years. Being an equipment geek, I was very unhappy with a lot of the gear my band members were using; cheap instruments and amps that sounded terrible, never worked correctly, and had the side effect of making the band sound terrible. So slowly but surely I purchased new instruments, amps, a PA, new lights, etc., that the other guys could use at rehearsal and at the shows. All this gear was stored in my rented space. As time went on, I wanted to get into making demos, so I borrowed a few grand from my dad and purchased a Pioneer quarter-inch four-track tape deck, and a Teac Model 5 console, and started recording demos for my band. A short while after that, my band decided to call it quits. Go figure . . . ha!

Being that I had purchased all this gear, signed a five-year lease on the room, and just bought the new recording equipment, I decided to open the place up to other bands for rehearsal and recording. In a few months, I was booked as much as I wanted to be. The place was a hit. This is where I learned, from trial and error, the basics of recording. About a year after I opened the joint up to the public, I got an offer from one of the bands that rehearsed there about four times a week to actually purchase the place from me. They thought it would be cheaper in the long run to own the place instead of paying me for time. So we agreed on a price that included the business, the lease, and the rehearsal gear, and I kept all the recording equipment and mics. After that I moved a few miles away and opened a new studio, bigger and better.

(As a side note, this first place under the record store was where the band Anthrax started, they would rehearse there a few times a week, and it was where I did all the demos for Paul Caravello who later became the drummer known as Eric Carr in Kiss.)

How do you balance producing and engineering in the studio? Give some key elements on keeping a session intact when dealing with artists.

First, I think you have to assess each particular session. What I mean is there has to be a dedicated producer, someone hired by the band or the label that has a vision and will oversee the project and keep things running smoothly, not just someone (or all) the band members calling themselves producers. Once you have figured this out, you can then get a sense of what your role is going to be for that particular session. Either you are going to be just the engineer trying to capture whatever it is the producer is looking for, or an engineer that has to help the band achieve their goal, quietly assuming the producer's role while not really getting the credit for doing such. But that's okay, it's part of the job as I see it.

I've found that once I gained the trust of the artist or band, then my role as an engineer was often expanded to include a lot of what a producer does, for example, working out the proper arrangement of the songs, tempos, keys, which instruments and amps to use on what parts, etc. Often the line between engineering and producing was blurred . . . but like I said earlier, this is just the norm, and I believe you'd get the same answer from any engineer who has been in the business long enough, I think they would all pretty much agree with this.

What is your trick on miking drums when recording?

Well, I'm not sure I have a trick for miking a drum kit. But here's what I usually do.

Number one: First, we'll set up the kit in the room, find a good spot for the set, depending on the sound we are after.

For example, should the drums be really live and roomy, dark, bright and crisp, or maybe really dead? The songs dictate the sonics I will be going after. Anyhow, once that is determined, we set up the kit, and listen to it in the spot chosen. Also it's important to remember that if you are cutting drums as part of an ensemble, there are good sight lines to the rest of the band, so this needs to be considered when setting the drums up in the room. Of course, if you are cutting drums to existing tracks, or by themselves, then this isn't a factor.

Number two: At this point I would determine if we need to replace any skins, bad or dead heads, and then we go to tuning. This is usually up to the drummer, how he or she likes the kit to sound, but I'm there to help make sure all the pieces fit to sound like one cohesive instrument. 'Cause if the set isn't tuned, then no matter what else you do, the drums will sound terrible. And since I am not a person to use samples or triggers, the drums need to sound great when we print them. (Note: if the tracks are mixed elsewhere, then I have no control of what they do, but if I'm mixing a project I have recorded, it's all the real drums sounds, nothing more!)

Number three: Okay, so now that we have the kit in position, all tuned and ready to go, it's time to determine what cymbals to use. Once again I defer to the drummer, *but* sometimes as with the kit, the drummer has chosen cymbals that work live but sound really nasty in a recorded situation. So once again we listen and try to figure out what works best in the room we are working in, as well as what best suits the song. I know this sounds tedious but after a while it's usually obvious what will work and what won't; it really becomes second nature.

Number four: Now we are ready to mic things up. I'll say it again, but the type of music/song we are recording will determine the miking method chosen for each particular session. That being said, I'm an old school kind of guy who likes to keep things very, very simple. So for example, if I'm tracking metal drums that need to cut through a mix, then I will go about miking every drum closely, trying to minimize leakage from the other drums the best I can; this can be especially hard with double bass drums, and maybe four to six toms. But it can be done, with the proper mics and placement; it just takes a bit of practice to learn what to use and where to put them. But on the other hand, if I was cutting rock, blues, or jazz drums, I'd be going with a very minimalist approach, using as few mics as possible to obtain the desired sound, and placing them slightly further away from each drum, allowing each sound to develop a bit more: a much more natural approach.

Depending on the music, and whether or not each drum is going to an individual track or being bussed together to only a few tracks, this would determine if I use EQ at all during tracking. I hardly use any EQ while tracking drums; I'd rather change the instrument and or the microphone, or its position before I go to an equalizer. Although with stuff like metal drums and the like, you do need to EQ certain elements like the "click-y" kick sound just to achieve the desired effect. This way upon playback you can hear all the intricacies the drummer has performed. But for most of the other types of music, I rarely EQ on the way in but maybe use a bit of high end on the snare. If the drums were to be bussed together like the entire kit to two tracks, then I would definitely EQ to achieve the sound I want, as there will be no real way to change things once combined without affecting everything else in that drum mix.

What advice can you give the novice home engineers on getting good-sounding tracks?

This is kind of obvious, but let's define the separate elements required to achieve the best-sounding tracks.

The musicians

He or she should be able to perform on their instrument as required. *It all starts here.* Now obviously sometimes this is not in our power to change, but let's face it: I don't care what follows this first, most important part of the signal chain; without this nothing else really matters, does it? So for argument's sake, we will assume the musicians are as good as they need to be to perform on their particular instruments.

The instrument

After the musician, what's next in line, you need a decent-sounding (working) instrument, whatever it is. More often than not, artists will enter a studio with an improperly maintained instrument. This could be a guitar with bad strings, or maybe intonation problems that won't allow it to be tuned, or stay in tune up and down the neck. Or a drummer who has his kit outfitted with dead old skins, 'cause they cost too much to replace, or the squeaky hi-hat or kick drum pedals . . . the list goes on and on. This is so common, although it seems obvious to us but is not always to the musicians that use these instruments live, and never really heard what they sound like until the first playback, and at that point it's too late!

Microphones

I would suggest buying the best mic(s) you can afford for the types of things you want to capture. We are really lucky today that there are so many great affordable mics out there to choose from. Do some research, whether on the net, or talk to other engineers you know and trust, and find out what best suits your particular needs. Sometimes you can rent and/or borrow a mic to try before you buy, which is always a good thing. And as long as it fits your budget, go for it.

Mic pre-amp/equalizer

Once again as with the mics, there is a plethora of mic pre-amps and equalizers out today that are amazing. As suggested above, I'd do a lot of research and purchase one or as many of the best you can afford for the type(s) of music you have chosen to work on. Remember, this is also a very important part of the signal chain and retaining the sound that starts in front of the mic. For equalizers, you need to decide what works best for you—do you want very broad strokes for sweetening, or something that gives you surgical precision? Only you can decide. Sometimes a combination of both is what's required, but it depends on what you are looking to achieve, and the way you work.

Converters

Last but not least, this is the final (some would argue the most important) stage in retaining the sonics you set out to capture when listening to the musician play their instrument. What can I say, you need to do the research and figure out what's within your budget, how many channels you need to track with . . . and buy the *best* you can afford. Remember, everything you record will probably pass through this converter stage at least once, so they better sound good, cause this will impart its sound on everything you record. And if you are mixing with a console or hybrid, you will be passing through this converter again.

And I think I would have to say, respect the music as best you can. I try to stay away from doing anything that is *not* required to achieve the desired results. I've always found that less is more. Do what's necessary, but nothing more, to the sound!

Mixing is always the issue for home recording engineers because of the limitations of their DAW. What advice can you give to those who mix in the box?

Okay, now ya got me . . . I'm sorry but I really can't answer this, as I have *no* real-world experience with mixing in the box, and I have *never* mixed a damn thing in the box, *ever*. And if I can help it, I never will. Been recording and mixing now for forty years, and I guess I'm stuck doing things the old way.

Everything I've done, no matter what it's been recorded to—tape, Pro Tools, Digital Performer, or in my case I've used iZ RADAR exclusively for the last eighteen years—has been broken out and mixed through a console or some sort of summing mixer with a ton of analog outboard gear.

I'm sure it's cool, and the benefits of total recall are obvious, but for me there is nothing like sitting in front of an analog console, and working the EQ's faders, etc. It's just tactile and real, and I love it. Not sure I could sit in front of a screen all day, work a mouse, and have the same level of enjoyment as I do now!

It's funny, one of my students said to me that mixing on my Trident console was so much easier and intuitive than mixing on his laptop with a mouse, the only way he has ever known. Do you find that the new generation has become too reliant on computers to do the work for them when it comes to recording and mixing?

I think the computer as a recording device is wonderful. Even though I don't really use them, the workstations like PT and what they can do to audio is mind-boggling. I mean, who woulda thunk?

It is an absolutely amazing time. That being said, if you check out some of the recording forums, you get the sense that a lot of the new generation of engineers are more interested in what the newest software release can do—you know the tricks, effects, pitch correction, beat detective—as well as all the new plug-ins offered. It seems like a lot of them are missing the point. I get songs to mix all the time from four- or five-piece rock bands where there are more than 120 tracks per song. And when I open the project up, there will be EQ, compressors, effects, and what have you on almost every damn track, sometimes two of each on a given track. The gain staging is completely messed up; things are so outta whack it's absurd. Plus, hardly anything is labeled correctly—I mean what does guitar track thirty-two really mean to me? I mean, really, are 120-plus tracks necessary for a simple rock tune? Do the rock records today really sound any better or capture more emotion then the best of the records from the '70s? Sure, we have better signal to noise, and wider bandwidth, no pops and clicks (which is great!) but you know what I'm talking about, the raw emotional impact of the music the first time you heard it. It was real, and made you never forget it. I can sum it up like this, back when The Beatles, The Stones, Zep, etc. cut records on four, eight, or sixteen tracks, the music was visceral and still is to this day, but for some reason, most of what is being released today isn't hitting me the same way. Go figure!

SYLVIA MASSY *INTERVIEW*

Figure 3.10 Sylvia Massy doo-dah!

Awesome girl power! I love seeing women engineering and producing; there are just not enough in the industry. I have two little girls and a son who I would like to see one day engineering or producing in the studio. Sylvia is a Grammy-winning producer and engineer for her work with Tool, System of a Down, Johnny Cash, and Prince. She's received over twenty-five gold and platinum records including awards for her work with the Red Hot Chili Peppers, Sevendust, and Tom Petty. You go, girl!

Give us a little background on how you got started in studio recording, becoming entranced with engineering.

I never went to school for engineering, it is something I learned by volunteering my time and by talking my way into studio sessions.

I like music and musicians and we speak the same language: the *dubba-dubba-cha* of the drummer, the *jung-gung-gung* of the guitarist and the *heeeellll-yeahhh* of the vocalist. I fit right in to the recording studio! I learned quickly and soon was producing within the first year. That doesn't mean I started making money right away . . . it took another ten years before that happened.

How do you balance producing and engineering in the studio? Give some key elements on keeping a session intact when dealing with artists.

The musician's ego is a sensitive one. Never let on that you might actually be a better player than they are, this will crush them. Encourage them to do their best performance, and then fix it after they leave the room . . . hahaha! Nah, really, it is not all that bad, I am blessed to be able to work with the best musicians the world has to offer. Seriously, I engineer when I need to now, but prefer to work with an engineer that knows my style. That way I can have a real connection with the musician.

What is your trick on miking drums when recording?

It's all about the phase because 'phase is God.' I use simple inexpensive mics, mostly dynamicZs on drums. I try to have them basically pointing in the same direction, to reduce the phase cancellation that will make your drums sound papery. I'll have top and bottom snare and tom mics that are set out of phase. The top mic gives you the attack, the bottom mic gives you the tone of the drum. Blend accordingly depending on what type of sound you are going for. Cymbals get condensers for the sparkle and I usually use a pair of large diaphragms overhead. I will take the extra time to listen to the kick mic soloed with every other drum mic, to identify any phasing issues, then I do the same thing with the snare. Correct phase is truly the secret to having big powerful drum sounds, even when you have several mics on a kit. Listen to the drums on those Tool records and you'll know what I mean.

What advice can you give the novice home engineers on getting good-sounding tracks?

Well, a crappy song won't sound good no matter how you record it . . . remember that! Beyond that, I suggest investing in a pair of good studio monitors, good mic pres, and good compressors. As far as mics go, start with a pair of Shure SM58s. They are extremely versatile for drums, vocals, guitars, and pretty much whatever else you can throw at them. Get used to recording with Pro Tools. Then you'll have everything you need to record. Now you need to go get the right material.

Mixing is always the issue for home recording engineers because of the limitations of their DAW. What advice can you give to those who mix in the box?

Don't be afraid to do side-by-side comparison listens with commercial music you admire. Take some time to set up a system where you can actually A/B your material with the stuff that was mixed by the pros. This will give you a chance to "reverse engineer" what they did to achieve their sound. You will be able to learn from listening carefully and emulate the compression, EQ, effects, etc. It gives you a chance to find limitations in your system, and where you can make up for those limitations by investing in additional plug-ins if needed. If you can, send your mix out into an external stereo compressor, then back into the box when printing. The stereo compressors can be pricey, but a box like a Manley Variable MU can make a huge difference in your finished mix. Another option is to send your mix to an outside mastering engineer, and cross your fingers that you'll get back what you intended.

It's funny, one of my students said to me that mixing on my Trident console was so much easier and intuitive than mixing on his laptop with a mouse, the only way he has ever known. Do you find that the new generation has become too reliant on computers to do the work for them when it comes to recording and mixing?

Mixing in the box can take the heart right out of the music. I still love using my Neve 8038 because it doesn't get in the way! Like driving a car, I don't need to look at the gearshift or the foot pedals; I can keep my eyes on the road! It is a very natural thing, grabbing a fader or several faders at the same time. I can put together a finished mix in very few passes, because I'm adjusting the entire board during those passes, not just one tedious track at a time.

I hope anyone chained to a laptop and a mouse will get a chance to try an analog board. Computer recording in combination with an analog front-end and an analog-mixing surface is a super-powerful way to work: fast and versatile. You can maintain the song's entire landscape as you detail and add each element into the mix.

MARK LINETT, YOUR PLACE OR MINE RECORDING *INTERVIEW*

Figure 3.11 Mark Linett and his studio toys!

Mark Linett has received Grammys for recording with such acts as Sugarland, Linkin Park, U2, Avril Lavigne, Fall Out Boy, Sheryl Crow, The Hives, Brian Wilson, Alanis Morissette, Aretha Franklin, and Duran Duran, to name a few. He started early in his career mixing live sound for Frank Zappa and went on to work at Sunset Sound in Los Angeles as a staff engineer. Through his diverse career in the music industry, he shares his stories and insights on what made him the engineer he is today.

Give us a little background on how you got started in studio recording, becoming entranced with engineering.

I was born in 1952, so rock and roll music was always a big part of my life. I remember listening to Elvis 45s at a friend's house on one of those RCA record players made just for a stack of singles. A few years later I vividly remember hearing The Beach Boys for the first time at another friend's house, those records belonging to his older sister. I was always fascinated with the amazing sound of rock records, and started buying them when I was maybe ten years old. My dad had a big Bell & Howell mono tape recorder and a pretty fancy "hi-fi" system, and I used to record music off the radio and off our television. Back then the whole process of how records were made was very mysterious and exciting, and I grew up wanting to know how such amazing sounds were recorded and pressed onto all the 45s I was buying. Just after I graduated from high school I started a concert sound company with a friend and for the next two years did a lot of shows with acts like Sha Na Na, Seals and Crofts, Livingston Taylor, and The Manhattan Transfer. Giving up that business, I moved to Los Angeles in 1972 and got a job at a small studio called Artist Recording in Hollywood. It wasn't a very good studio, but I did get to do a lot of recording. What was lacking was a mentor, someone who knew how to make records properly, to show me the right way to do things. I did have the first records I engineered released, but after two years I moved to Boston to go back to school. It was there through a strange set of circumstances that I ended up getting a job mixing live sound for Frank Zappa. I did two tours with him, and when he wasn't touring I took his sound and light production on tour with other acts like ELO. From there I went on the mix for Earth, Wind & Fire and later Journey. It was through EWF that I met their studio engineer George

Massenburg who helped me get a job as a staff engineer at Sunset Sound, a world-class studio here in Los Angeles. At Sunset I finally got to work as an assistant to many talented engineers and producers, learning an amazing amount in the process, and it was there that I began to engineer sessions for artists like America, Hall & Oates, and Jimmy Webb. Leaving Sunset around 1980, I got a job as staff engineer at Warner Records Amigo Studios, where I got to engineer records for numerous artists including Randy Newman, Los Lobos, Rickie Lee Jones, and Michael McDonald. When the studio closed in 1984, I went independent, eventually building my own studio and remote truck. In 1987 a random call to a studio to book time resulted in an offer to engineer a last-minute session for Brian Wilson, and so began a relationship with him and The Beach Boys that continues to this day.

How do you balance producing and engineering in the studio? Give some key elements on keeping a session intact when dealing with artists.

The biggest difference is simply that as producer you have the right and responsibility to work with the artist to get the best out of their material, from the arrangement to the performance.

What is your trick on miking drums when recording?

Over the years I have done a variety of things when recording drums. For a long time I used a stereo ribbon mic for overheads, as well as ribbon mics for the toms. These days I use Sony C-38s for overheads and AKG D-190s for toms, and I always have several room mics including at least one cheap "junk" mic, which I heavily compress.

What advice can you give the novice home engineers on getting good-sounding tracks?

Use your ears and experiment. Since so much recording is done "off the clock," you are free to try different things, but I should also emphasize the value of a spontaneous musical performance. You can't let getting the sound affect the music or you won't get the best from the musicians.

Mixing is always the issue for home recording engineers because of the limitations of their DAW. What advice can you give to those who mix in the box?

It's really all the same, in or out of the box—you need to use your ears and learn what can be done to improve the recorded sounds and make it all fit together. That being said, mixing in the box offers so many ways to process, fix, and improve things that the choices are almost endless.

It's funny, one of my students said to me that mixing on my Trident console was so much easier and intuitive than mixing on his laptop with a mouse, the only way he has ever known. Do you find that the new generation has become too reliant on computers to do the work for them when it comes to recording and mixing?

Well, using a console is much more tactile than trying to mix with a mouse, and when I work in the box I always use some sort of control surface to control Pro Tools so I can still "feel" the mix.

HAL LINDES OF DIRE STRAITS *INTERVIEW*

Figure 3.12 Hal Lindes, guitarist from the super group Dire Straits and award-winning film composer!

My good friend and guitar-shredding buddy Hal Lindes is a class act. Hal joined Dire Straits at the end of 1980 and had a five-year tenure with the band. He joined during the tour of their third album, *Making Movies*. Then he was featured on their next album, 1982's *Love Over Gold*, as well as the 1983 EP titled *ExtendedancEPlay*, and the 1984 album *Alchemy Live*, a double album of excerpts from concerts at the Hammersmith Odeon in July, 1983. Hal has won various music awards for composing music for both film and television, like the Royal Television Society Award for the British Academy of Film and Television Arts (BAFTA) for *Reckless* and a Television and Radio Industries Club (TRIC) award for Best TV Theme Music. Hal also composed the soundtrack to *The Boys Are Back*, a Miramax film directed by Scott Hicks and starring Clive Owen. In *The Boys Are Back*, Hal's guitar score is used with music from the popular Icelandic band Sigur Rós. *Variety* magazine states, "A selection of tracks by popular Icelandic band Sigur Rós adds emotional ballast and nicely complements Hal Lindes's score." We have played on so many songs together for the Guitar Master Series I've lost count, but he has such a great feel for the guitar and we always seem to complement the song and each other.

Give us a little background on how you put together your home studio and for what purpose—composing, recording live musicians, etc.

Going back to the Dire Straits days, the studio was put together for writing and demo-ing songs. Over time it has evolved to cover the needs of both composing for film and writing/recording songs. I like to think of it as an all-purpose recording studio that's been highjacked by a resident film composer. The mixing console is long gone, replaced by a host of mic pres, mainly vintage Neve 1073s, 1272s, 33122a's and APIs. The mics generally run through the Neves, a little compression may be added to the recording chain but it's just to tickle the meters. The mic pres run into Apogee A to D converters that bring the digital signal into the computer. The studio has the capability to record a small band, but usually it's just one or two musicians at a time. My desert island mic would be the u47. On the film composing side, a Mac Pro runs Logic Audio, and Mac Minis run the plug-in sample libraries.

What is your studio setup, DAW, plug-ins, and do you use any analog gear?

I'm a longtime Logic Audio user, going back to when it was C-Lab Notator running on an Atari 1040ST with a whopping 512kb of RAM (the ST was the first home computer with integrated MIDI support). Sadly, Logic seems to have lost its way somewhat, becoming less of a pro user application and more of a casual hobbyist, Garage Band type of application. An entire career's worth of music files are vested in Logic, so I'm reluctant to make a change at this point, but having said that, a change to Cubase and away from the Mac platform may be on the horizon. Most folks out there are working from pretty much the same sonic palette of "in-the-box" plug-ins. To avoid swimming in the same generic pool, I feel it is vital to mix things up by using as much outboard gear as possible. Outboard gear adds richness and a bigger dimension to the sound that is missing from working solely "in the box." For reverb, I like to mix Logic's PlatinumVerb with the Lexicon LX-300 and PCM-70. Outboard echoes include a Roland SDE 3000 and an analog SRE 555 tape delay. For compression it's the Urei 1176 and the Altec 436c with the EMI RS124 mod. A pair of Neve 1073s and Altec 436c's generally gets strapped across the stereo mix bus, adding a sparkle and a shimmer that brings the mixes to life. The Adrena-Linn and Korg A3 are also fun boxes to have kicking around. The brilliant Robert Hovland services all the studio tube gear and Toby Foster looks after the microphones. Toby possesses a great ability to modify dull, lackluster mics into something splendid. The Neve guru Avedis looks after the Neve gear.

When you record, how do you balance being an artist and an engineer? Give some key elements on keeping a session intact.

That's a great question, Brian. It's definitely a bit of a juggling act, because as you know being an artist and being an engineer are two completely different skill sets. When I first started writing film scores, my studio had a physical mixer, and there was much more time to compose the music. I would bring in an engineer for the tracking sessions and for the final music mixes. With Dire Straits, I watched some of the great giants of recording engineers at work first hand. As a film composer, I've had the good fortune to work with the highly talented John Mackswith, who was part of my team for many years. Through them all, I learned the majority of what I know today about how to capture a sound onto tape, how to record instruments, which mic to use and where to place the microphones. John is the master of tweaking reverbs and delays to get gorgeously evocative sounds and I try to emulate that. Time restraints and budgets being what they are today, and working mostly "in the box" at breakneck speeds to get the music cues and revisions delivered on time, it's simply more efficient to engineer the sessions and mix the music myself, usually mixing the music simultaneously as it's being composed. It's a matter of having to wear two hats at the same time, and it can be a tricky thing trying to achieve a great guitar performance while simultaneously watching the meters.

Being a composer, what virtual instruments do you find have the most useful tools when scoring and why?

To accomplish the somewhat daunting task of writing film music under a tight deadline, the key for me is to get any ideas down as fast as possible. In the initial stages, if I find myself trawling through acres of plug-in libraries to hunt down that perfect sample, the inspiration for the music will vanish back into the ether. In order to get the idea down fast, I work with a writing palette of rough sounds that can be accessed quickly, knowing that they will be replaced with better sounds or live players at a later stage. The commercial sample libraries are getting bigger and better all the time, so there's plenty of stuff out there to create great-sounding scores. I tend to mix the newer plug-in libraries with some of the older Akai and Emu libraries which have been converted for use with Logic's EXS. There's a musicality and character to some of those older, smaller samples that just can't be beat by the newer multi-miked, heavily sampled libraries. I create a fair amount of my own samples as well, with a growing personal guitar library. I'm also a big fan of using the older MIDI gear like the Ensoniq MR, Roland 5080, and Kurzweil PC88.

As a guitarist, how do you record your guitar tracks—live with miking an amp or do you use an amp simulator?

I pretty much record guitars with either an amp or DI. Rarely is an amp simulator used unless I'm looking for a specific effect. If I'm in a hurry to get a part down, I might just record the guitar DI and re-amp at a later time. As for amp choices, one of my favorites is a Fender Vibrolux, particularly for those big, clean classic Fender tones. If I'm looking for more crunch or drive, I'll go for a smaller amp like a Fender Harvard or a Fender Champ style amp. For more character it's hard to beat an old Valco or '50s Rickenbacker amp. The amps are usually miked with an SM57 and a tube condenser like a U67. If I'm looking for more of a trashy lo-fi tone, I might try something like a Russian Octava MK-012.

LARRY CRANE, *TAPE OP* MAGAZINE *INTERVIEW*

Figure 3.13 Larry Crane from *Tape Op* magazine

Larry is the self-proclaimed engineer guru who founded the esoteric recording magazine *Tape Op*, and owns Jackpot! Recording Studio in the soggy Northwest town of Portland, Oregon. Deeply seated in the alternative rock scene, he engineers bands such as Elliott Smith, Sleater-Kinney, The Go-Betweens, The December-ists, and Jason Lytle. Though these bands are very remote from the well-known acts of other interviews, it is an interesting view on how underground engineers approach recording music with their own style and flair.

Give us a little background on how you got started in studio recording, becoming entranced with engineering.

I started recording me and my friends in high school. I released cassettes of this stuff in the early '80s. In the mid '80s, I ended up in an "alternative rock" band and we made four albums, working with two different engineers/producers. I enjoyed being part of that process, and recorded my band's demos and guided the studio process. A year or so after that band ended, I started recording in my home, and a few years later quit my day job and moved into a commercial space as Jackpot! Recording Studio. I never meant to do this as a job, but many of my musician friends had faith in me and talked me into doing this.

How do you balance producing and engineering in the studio? Give some key elements on keeping a session intact when dealing with artists.

I feel the engineering side is the easy, any-monkey-could-learn-this part. It really isn't that hard once you learn some basics, and if you learn how to listen, you'll know what to do. But producing, creatively guiding an album project to becoming far better than any-one even imagined, is much harder and requires many skills. I focus on everything: how things sound, takes, tempo, vibe, feelings, mood, performance, pitch, phrasing, arrangement, key, etc. You can't know all, but most artists bring stuff to the table that needs work. Arrange-ment of song parts and how all the layers of instruments fit together is very important to me, more so than how things are recorded.

What is your trick on miking drums when recording?

Phase, phase, and phase. Keep it in phase! Drum selection and tuning is key. Rooms that don't get too live or too choked down when a drummer is playing are important. The right part of a room for placement is important. Proper gain staging and headroom are very important. You can ruin a snare transient so easily, and while compressors are fun, be sure of what you might be committing to. Oh, miking drums? Should be easy if you get all that other stuff right!

What advice can you give the novice home engineers on getting good-sounding tracks?

Learn how to REALLY listen to the tracks you are recording. Learn how to decide if the tracks are working together or fighting each other and why. Learn how to predict how all the needed tracks of a song will fit together. Challenge yourself: record a song using four tracks no matter how many you have. Record every instrument and vocal live on a song to two tracks. Record and mix without plug-ins. Try to limit your options and come up with other ways to solve problems. The biggest problem I see most of the time is that home recordings are in bad rooms, with bad reflections. Learn how to hear these reflections! Buy some quality speakers and a great monitor controller and DAC. Otherwise you are hearing and learning nothing.

Mixing is always the issue for home recording engineers because of the limitations of their DAW. What advice can you give to those who mix in the box?

Don't mix in the box. Hire a pro, like me! Really, all kidding aside, a pro who has a great track record in mixing records in a similar style to yours will be able to fix all the problems you may have introduced while recording. They will understand what balances will work best, and they will make your recording sound great. If you really want to mix it yourself, then good luck. It took me years to feel I was sort of okay at it. How are you going to succeed on this one project? Likely you won't. No offense, but I am sent hundreds of records like this every year. I can usually guess that it was recorded by the bass player in a practice room and mixed at his or her home on poor quality speakers. It sounds like a demo. Is that what you want?

It's funny, one of my students said to me that mixing on my Trident console was so much easier and intuitive than mixing on his laptop with a mouse, the only way he has ever known. Do you find that the new generation has become too reliant on computers to do the work for them when it comes to recording and mixing?

I like the fact that I can edit and automate tracks and not have to perform a mix. I always hated that! I want to come up with the solution and solve the problem and be done and have it not repeat. I used to print tracks back to another tape track and do my edits or such so I could be "done." So, in my mind, relying on computers isn't bad. It's only a tool. But when I open a "failed" mix session that someone is unhappy with and I see millions of automated fader moves, ten plug-ins on each channel, and 100 aux channels, I know what is wrong. I remove all that crap, do a few simple things, and the mix is better. Someone was "reliant" in the completely wrong way!

Chapter 4

Recording Tracks

I remember, as an adolescent in the '70s, recording guitar parts on my dad's Grundig two-track quarter-inch reel-to-reel tape machine, using a razor to edit the tape—which I still do today. That's right. I find it necessary, for certain types of music, to record to two-inch tape, especially when tracking drums, and bass and rhythm guitars.

But today, of course, all one has to do is buy a computer, Mac or PC, and there are a plethora of digital recording platforms that come complete with tons of music loops to help you create songs. This takes the worry out of the recording process, letting the artist concentrate on the actual music at hand and not so much on the technical aspect of it. But with all of this high-tech freedom to create, you still can't overlook some essential areas.

TIPS AND TRICKS

To help you get better results for your DIY recording projects, here are some tips and tricks that always work for me.

Combine both the analog and digital worlds

Even with the convenience of using built-in samples and recording everything in the "box," I find you need to combine both the analog and the digital worlds. That's why I mix everything out of Pro Tools or Logic through my analog classic Trident recording console and use physical outboard gear, like Urei 1176, LA-4, and so on.

Though an indie artist does not have to go to that extent, if you want to record guitar, I strongly recommend recording it from an amp with a very affordable mic, like a Shure SM57. Direct guitar signals are not very pleasing to listen to and many of the plug-ins have a processed sound.

Before I had a recording studio, I recorded guitar cabinets with an SM57 in my apartment in Los Angeles; I would place the amp in a closet, so as not to disturb the neighbors. To an all-digital song, this brings the track alive with an actual live instrument.

Keep in mind, if you want to change the tone of the instrument, then move the mic first before you reach for any of your EQ plug-ins. Usually, this is the most natural and effective way.

Invest in tools of the trade

You would be surprised how many instruments the SM57 can record—everything imaginable. For less than a hundred bucks this is the most versatile microphone a musician can own, being able to record everything from horns to drums. There are also companies like CAD, Nady, and Audix that make affordable mic sets for drums as well. Plus, depending on your digital interface you may want to use a mic preamp, which, again, a plethora of companies make from ninety-nine bucks to thousands. One of my favorites is the Universal Audio 610.

But remember, you don't have to break the bank to get pro audio equipment today; there are so many affordable companies that manufacture gear for every price range. Bear in mind, this is a one-time expense for an essential item that you can use for many projects. If you plan on recording music as your livelihood, this is a good investment.

Don't drown under too many tracks

This is an area where I see so many musicians drown themselves. Just because you can have unlimited tracks doesn't mean you have to use tons of tracks for a song. If the song really calls for many tracks and crossfades, okay, then go ahead. But I still like the track limitation we had in the past—there was no choice but to stop recording take after take—simply because you would run out of tracks. Decisions had to be made when the take was completed so you could then move on.

Believe me, after twenty years of doing this, 99.9 percent of the time the best takes are usually within the first three; after that you can hear musicians start to wane. I advise you to label every track, such as Bass 1, Bass Chorus, Sax Solo, and so on; otherwise during mix down you'll waste way too much time searching for the correct tracks to mix. There is nothing worse than having forty-five tracks staring at you, unlabeled, for a five-minute song, in which you have to determine how to reconfigure the whole song.

Don't crush the living essence out of your mix to make it loud

Man, when the Waves L2 Processor came out, yes it made everything loud, but it destroyed so many mixes just for the sake of loudness! Music has to have some sort of dynamics, not just soaring levels constantly in the red. This is why vinyl has been making a comeback in recent years, especially the old recordings, like David Bowie's *Diamond Dogs*, *Led Zeppelin IV*, etc.—those records possess dynamics, no matter how much they rock out. Hell, even the hair bands had dynamics in their mixes.

If you crush the living essence out of your mix and make it loud, you'll lose all of the tone of the instruments and vocals. But fortunately there is a great, affordable mastering plug-in that doesn't squash your mix and still keeps it alive: the Slate Digital FG-X. For two hundred bucks this plug-in is terrific. It keeps your dynamics in place and still gives you the loudness you need for modern-sounding tracks.

Bottom line

Today's musician can be it all: the engineer, producer, and artist all in the confines of their own home. So use the technology to your advantage and take your time when recording to get the performances correct. And always be well rehearsed before you hit that red button!

MICROPHONE PRE-AMPS

Neve 1081

Rupert Neve needs no introduction, but for those of you who are not familiar with the 1081, it is probably one of the most desirable mic pres in the recording world. It was originally designed in 1972 as the mic/line pre-amp and equalizer section for the Neve modular console. These consoles are still being used today on platinum-selling albums, and for good reason. Rupert himself won a technical Grammy from the National Academy of Recording Arts and Sciences for his contributions to outstanding technical significance in the recording field. The 1081 modules are still built by hand in Burnley, United Kingdom, under the mother company AMS in much the same manner as the original modules, using the original components, hand-wound transformers, and time-honed construction methods.

The 1081's magic is in its Neve equalization, which features effective high- and low-pass filters designed to separate unwanted signals. The flexibility of shaping your sound is so intuitive that creating curves and slopes can be achieved at a high artistic level. This explains the longtime love affair with the Neve recording console for the past forty years. It is still an exceptional choice for recording guitars and is the original rock-n-roll pre-amp made to rock!

BAE 1073 Mic Pre

This is a sweet-sounding mic pre based on the classic Neve 1073. It uses the same 283 card and transformers as the original for a fraction of the cost. For those of you who are doing digital recording only, this is a must-have mic pre for guitar! It adds warmth to the guitar tone and fattens up the overall sound. It has a very present tone, so you really hear the attack of the pick and fingers on the fretboard without having to compress. It adds sub harmonics to the bottom end, making it feel large without the mud, and it adds silkiness to the high frequencies, giving it sheen. It has a red gain knob and a gray output. Every click on the gain knob is a five dB increment, so you can always adjust the output level to get in between the five dB steps. With its large headroom, it is an excellent choice for the low-output ribbon microphones.

SSL 4000

Many consider this to be the Holy Grail of consoles because of its clarity and groundbreaking automation. Virtually all SSLs have been used on every pop album since the 1980s. Outside of the big-name studios that own one of these babies, purchasing one will certainly break the bank. At close to $100,000 brand new, and with a vintage one costing a fortune to repair, you may want to just go the cost-effective route and purchase an SSL Mynx with 9K Series Mic Pre and Dynamics Modules. For a fraction of the price, you can still have the SSL legendary technology that is perfect as an interface with your favorite DAW.

SSL Mynx uses the identical circuit design and manufacturing of Duality and AWS 900+ consoles. The Mynx is a desktop mini X-Rack that allows you to load various X-Rack modules into two slots. The SSL Mic Pre module, with its compact size, is designed especially for the DAW user. The Mic Amp module has a great mic pre with seventy-five dB of gain, variable impedance control, phantom power and phase reverse line input with level control, front panel instrument input, and low and high pass filters. This is perfect for the guitarist who has a small home studio setup. SSL has always been known for a non-coloring sound, with audiophile clarity.

Universal Audio LA-610

One of my favorite mic pres is the UA 610, because of its tube warmth that adds to the guitar. It especially shines when used in recording guitar directly to hard disk. And you've got to dig those huge rotary knobs it sports.

The genius behind the 610, one of the first modular recording consoles in the world, was Bill Putnam, the man who has been aptly called "the father of modern recording." Interestingly enough, Putnam had several studios, including Universal Recording in Chicago and United/Western in Los Angeles, that used his early Universal Audio console designs.

The 610 was famous for its prominent preamplifier, featured on a plethora of classic recordings, from Frank Sinatra to Van Halen. The 610 Modular features variable gain and output levels, variable impedance switching, balanced line/Hi-Z inputs, and my favorite high and low shelving EQ. I find the EQ very useful in particular. It is subtle yet extremely musical and can shape a guitar tone nicely to sit in a track.

Focusrite ISA430

The twenty-five-year-old British company Focusrite manufactures this pre-amp. The shred maestro James Ryan's guitar approach utilizes the ISA430 MkII, which has analog channel strip technology, bringing together all the classic designs in one rack unit. The mic pre-amp section has an impedance switching and "mic air" effect (a wire-wound inductor for increased spaciousness), three compressor options (VCA, Vintage Opto, and Opto Limit) combined with the compressed/uncompressed, and even a blend feature.

Routing and monitoring are important features on the ISA430, which allows you to listen (hone in on the frequency you wish to affect) on compressor, gate, and expander circuits. To round things off, the ISA430 has a unique phase cancellation-based de-esser circuit and an optional twenty-four-bit/192-kHz high-performance stereo A-D converter, allowing you to retain your analog guitar signal into the digital domain. Focusrite has always been known for its digital clarity and multi-dynamic rack units.

Aside from the Neve 1081, these mic pre-amps are not terribly expensive, when you consider the high-priced boutique options out there in the recording retail world. Don't feel that you have to use some sort of guitar pod or a lame amp simulator plug-in to get your sound recorded. Purchase a good mic pre and a basic Shure 57 mic, and you'll be in business to record true guitar tone to your DAW. Believe me, there is nothing worse than hearing guitar parts recorded purely digital, thin and sterile—much like hearing drums recorded direct to hard disk. Take your time and get your sound together in the room before you record down.

Sometimes I see guitarists record both ways, which yields very good results. On one track they record a direct signal with a Line 6, and on another track they record a miked amp signal. One way to be sure of picking the right mic pre for you is to call a local rental company, such as SIR in New York, and rent a few pres for a day to see what floats your boat. This way you know what to buy, and you don't have to commit until you're positive of the result. Either way, get that guitar tone recorded and shred on!

JDK R20 Channel Mic Pre

I love a mic pre-amp with a VU meter so you know what kind of input/output is happening. This is a very well-made mic pre. And how can you go wrong with the design team of API behind it? With the pad switch attenuating the microphone signal by twenty dB (the instrument signal by ten dB) and the fifty-four dB of gain, this is a good choice for most microphones. Though some would say it's not enough gain for a ribbon mic, I've never had a problem miking a cabinet. It has a nice warm, transparent sound that leaves the precious guitar tone intact.

It's extremely easy to use with just a gain knob that determines your input/output signal. It has a smooth sound that captures the accurate guitar tone as you hear it in the room. This is a very different type of mic pre from the BAE 1073 because it is a transformerless mic pre-amp; the gain stage is directly wired as opposed to running through a transformer, common in classic mic pres. This makes it a very affordable and a fine choice for all types of guitars.

MICROPHONES

Choosing the right microphones

Van Halen fans have always wondered how longtime engineer Donn Landee recorded Eddie's trademark guitar tone. He had to admit that he used a cheap SM 57 mic on a Marshall cabinet. As some of you readers may know, the Shure 57 is a basic $89 mic that you can purchase at any local music store. This proves that you can get great tone without breaking the bank.

As an engineer, you need to understand the various dynamics that come from instruments you decide to record, e.g., a guitar and amp. For instance, when playing a Les Paul through a Marshall JCM800, you get a very compressed, overdriven rock tone, as opposed to playing a Strat through a Fender Super Reverb, which produces a more dynamic bluestone. Both can be recorded successfully with an SM 57, but if you want to spend a little bit more cash, you can buy what I refer to as a "57 on steroids," the Sennheiser 421 mic.

If you have more of a budget and you want to capture the sound of your amp in the room, you may want to try the Neumann TLM 103 or the more expensive TLM 49, which are both large-diaphragm cardioid microphones. The large diaphragm of the mic will capture the ambience of the room. In particular, the TLM 49 has a wonderful airiness to its recordings. By comparison, the 57 has a very small mic diaphragm, which is more beneficial for unidirectional close miking.

I'm sure some of you have heard the buzz about ribbon microphones, and yes, it is true that in some recording applications of guitars the ribbon mic is perfect for acoustic instrument replication. The Rolls Royce of ribbon mics is the Royer 121 or the famous Beatles BBC 4038. However, you can always go with the less expensive Beyerdynamic M160 mic and still get a great-sounding acoustic tone.

With any microphone you decide to go with, you'll have to experiment with placement techniques. Personally, I've had very good results recording acoustic guitars using the AKG C1000S, which I like to angle downward toward the fretboard side of the hole. Keep in mind that you may have to make some minor adjustments, depending on the size of the guitar body and your finger style.

I've been recording professionally for twenty-five years, and I am always trying to find new ways of achieving a great-sounding guitar tone. Just recently, I discovered a cool way to achieve stereo imaging by miking a single cabinet with two mics. First, close-mic one speaker between the cone and the edge with a Beyer M160 and far-mic the amp using a Neumann TLM 49 about five feet back, pointing the forty-nine directly at the Marshall insignia on the cabinet.

My baby is a Trident thirty-two-channel mixing console, in which I use one of the mic pres for the Neumann and use the Universal Audio 610 for the M160. I bus them both to tape or Pro Tools and hardpan one left and one right. I've always found that experimenting with different mics and amps in combination with your guitar style can really produce that hot buttah tone!

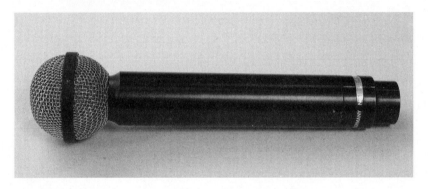

Figure 4.1 Beyerdynamic M160 ribbon microphone, excellent on guitar cabinets
Erik Christian Photography

Beyerdynamic M160

The M160 has to be one of my favorite guitar microphones. It's a very simple design but extremely effective for recording guitars. The mic's characteristics are very clean sounding, with a nice punch to the upper-mid frequencies. Because it is a ribbon mic, it really captures the nuances of the guitar and amp.

It's hard to believe that the company states that the manufacturing process for the M160 has remained fundamentally unchanged since the model was first introduced in 1957. Ironically, it was originally developed as an alternative to the then-expensive condenser microphone. Nowadays, it seems that ribbon microphones have made a huge comeback and have become well known for their accurate reproduction.

Figure 4.2 Royer R-101, great all-around ribbon Figure 8
Erik Christian Photography

Royer R-101

The R-101 is a mono, passive ribbon microphone utilizing an offset-ribbon transducer and a two-and-half-micron ribbon element. These microphones are considered to be the new breed of ribbon microphones, designed particularly for electric guitar cabinets. They feature an advanced multilayered windscreen for protection from air blasts and plosives, an internally shock-mounted ribbon transducer system, and a reduced proximity effect for closer miking with less bass buildup, especially on large amp cabinets.

Just place this mic as close as you like to the speaker and play loud and proud. I've used it on four-by-twelve cabinets, and they sound extremely good, keeping the full body of the sound without being too muddy. In combination with a Shure SM57 and a Sennheiser MD 421, you get a great combination of textures that can be blended in the final mix. The R-101 retains the midrange frequencies very well, creating a smooth response. They are also very good on acoustic guitar. The ribbon element responds very well, capturing the natural wood sound and the metallic ringing of the strings.

Figure 4.3 sE Voodoo VR1, wonderful natural
-sounding ribbon microphone, great on
horns
Erik Christian Photography

sE Voodoo VR1

The sE Voodoo has to be one of the nicest ribbon microphones on the market today. It performs across twenty Hz to twenty kHz, which is a direct result of the Rupert Neve collaboration with sE. This was made possible by using state-of-the-art transformers and a Rupert-designed circuit board to reveal HF (High Frequency), which is usually absent.

What you get is a whole new sound different from any other ribbon mic on the market. This enables the Voodoo to extend performance, which had not previously been possible, except in condenser microphones. I found it to have a fuller frequency range, and on a guitar cabinet, it really captures those mid- and high-range frequencies. The Voodoo really records the detail of the guitar, enabling you to hear the fingers on the fretboard. This makes the job of placing the guitar in the mix so much easier; the guitar stands out but has nice seating in the final mix. It's perfect on acoustic guitars, too, by placing the microphone by the twelfth fret pointing down toward the sound hole. It's great because there is no proximity effect, capturing the pristine-ness of the instrument.

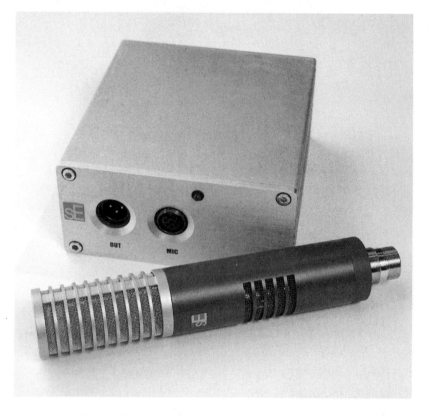

Figure 4.4 The wonderfully revealing sE Classic ribbon tube microphone
Erik Christian Photography

sE RT1 Ribbon Tube

The RT1 is probably one of the best ribbon tube microphones. Unlike other ribbon mics, in which you have to really push the gain on the pre-amp to get the output up, the RT1 has its own power supply. Thus, it has plenty of gain to print on tape directly!

I find it to be a very smooth microphone with the warmth of the tube, making it a real vintage piece right out of the box. It's absolutely fantastic on electric guitar cabinets, in any shape or size. Many times I record two amps at a time through the Framptone Amp Switcher, using the RT1 on a Soldano Reverb-O-Sonic four-by-twelve and a Sennheiser 421 on a Fender Showman four-by-twelve cabinet. For a clean-sounding strat tone, this microphone is the one. It adds a nice silky sheen to the recording without coloring the tone of the source. It's a real tone-capturing microphone for guitars!

Figure 4.5 Sennheiser e609, designed especially for miking guitar cabinets
Erik Christian Photography

Sennheiser e609

The Sennheiser e609 is able to withstand high SPLs (sound pressure levels) without distorting. Now that's what I want to hear. The 609 Silver's flat-profile capsule facilitates extremely close miking of guitar cabinets. This is a result from the super cardioid design that improves isolation especially in live sound and studio recording. This all creates a wider frequency response and an increased output, improving the overall performance.

Though the 609 does not have the articulation and dynamics that the new ribbon microphones have, it still records a fat sound from cabinets. The beauty of it is its simplicity and ease of use. This is a

113

perfect microphone when cutting tracks with a live band because of the super cardioid pickup pattern that provides isolation from other surrounding instrument signals. The 609 is great to use in conjunction with a ribbon mic such as the M160 when miking an open-back amp, such as the Fender Super Reverb.

Figure 4.6 AKG C414B-ULS, the best all-around microphone you can buy for your studio
Erik Christian Photography

AKG C414

The 414 is the mother ship of microphones. For more than sixty years, engineers and producers have used the 414 for almost every imaginable application. It has become the reference microphone for almost all comparative microphone tests and is one of the most used condenser microphones in the world. It boosts a gold-sputtered one-inch dual-diaphragm; a selectable cardioid of hyper cardioid, omnidirectional, or Figure-eight polar patterns; a two-stage pre-attenuation pad and bass cut filter; and a high sound pressure level capability of up to 160 dB SPL.

This is the real deal in studio microphones. It shines on so many instruments, from horns to acoustic guitar to overhead drum mics. I love it on acoustic guitar. With a little experimenting and moving it around in front of the guitar, you can get a really natural recording. I usually place it between the twelfth fret and the sound hole of the guitar pointing down toward the bridge.

Figure 4.7 SM57, the cheapest dynamic microphone on the market that can be used for many different applications
Erik Christian Photography

Shure SM57

What can be said about the Shure SM57 that hasn't already been said? This is the microphone you're sure to find in every live venue, recording studio, and school band room around the world. It is the true workhorse of microphones!

The SM57 is affordable and effective, and it loves electric guitar cabinets. Every guitarist should have at least one of these glued to his amp for backup. As you've seen throughout the book, the 57 is still the most popular mic used by both artists and engineers. An old favorite microphone combination is placing the 57 about an inch away from the center of the speaker cone and then combining it with a Sennheiser MD 421 on the right side of the 57 at a forty-five-degree angle and keeping it the same distance from the speaker. You can then record each mic on its own track and blend according to taste. You'll get a nice beefy tone. The 421 will provide the body of the tone, and the 57 will record the higher frequencies of the guitar, making it a perfect match.

Figure 4.8 Sennheiser MD 421, what I call a sure 57 on steroids!
Erik Christian Photography

Sennheiser MD 421

Put simply, the 421 is an SM57 on steroids. It's probably one of the most diverse mics ever made. It is most commonly used for miking toms, but it has so much more potential. In fact, the 421 shines in broadcasting applications, such as radio announcing, featuring the five-position bass control, which enhances its all-around qualities.

The wonderful advantage of the 421 is that it handles very high SPLs. It was born to be a rock guitar mic. Being a large-diaphragm dynamic microphone that came out originally in the early '60s, the 421 has been used on almost every classic rock recording in some way or another.

Figure 4.9 Neumann TLM 49, wonderful as a
room microphone or on acoustic guitar
Erik Christian Photography

Neumann TLM 49

The TLM 49 is a solid-state cardioid microphone with warm characteristics. I've used these mics on everything from guitar cabinets to sax, vocals, and even piano (in a stereo pair). I usually use it in conjunction with another mic when recording guitar cabinets. For instance, I'll near-mic a Marshall cabinet with an M 160 and place the TLM 49 about five feet back. You get a nice clear image with the M 160 and a thicker cabinet sound of the room with the TLM 49. I blend these two signals together during the mix, placing the M 160 signal a bit higher, while fading just enough of the TLM 149 to create a thicker depth of the guitar. Because the TLM 49 is a large-diaphragm microphone, I feel it captures a fuller, warmer sound of the guitar cabinets, creating a realistic recording of the sound you hear in the room.

Figure 4.10 AKG D112, a mainstay on kick drums, but also fantastic on bass amps
Erik Christian Photography

AKG D112

I use this method on many bass and kick drum recordings through the Radial J48 Direct Box as a buffer to split the signal. I plug the amp into the Radials through jack and plug the bass into the input. I'll then take the XLR signal directly to one track and print the miked signal.

This gives me the flexibility to blend the direct signal a little lower during mix down, which I find adds a full body to the bass sound. For solo bass tracks, it adds a wonderful depth of sound to the bass and gives the engineer flexibility when mixing. You can also do a nice stereo pan with the two signals, enabling you to EQ and affect the signals differently.

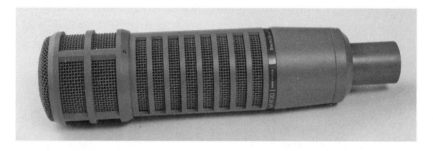

Figure 4.11 Electro-Voice RE20, killer on floor tom and kick drums
Erik Christian Photography

Electro-Voice RE20

Now the RE20 Variable-D dynamic cardioid microphone is truly an industry standard, but not as a guitar microphone. Instead it is used in the broadcast industry as an announcer mic. It features the EVs Variable-D design along with the heavy-duty internal P-pop filter, which reduces proximity effect. It's made like a brick house with an internal element shock-mount that reduces vibration noise. It even has a bass roll off-switch to use if things get too boom-y from the amp.

This is my designated mic for bass. I place it directly in front of the fifteen-inch bass cabinet speaker, a little offset from the voice coil. It adds no colorization to the tone and captures the bass quite accurately. The RE20 has always been popularly used to mic a kick drum and floor toms, again resulting in an excellent sound.

Figure 4.12 AKG C1000, a very good all-around microphone with a nine-volt battery
Erik Christian Photography

AKG C1000 S

Another extremely versatile microphone is the AKG C1000 S, ideally suited for all kinds of recording and live sound reinforcement. A standard nine-volt battery or the phantom power from a mixer can power the mic. What's very useful is that the polar pattern can quickly be switched from cardioid to hypercardioid simply by attaching the provided PPC 1000 Polar Pattern Converter to the microphone capsule. There is also an adapter, called the PB 1000 Presence Boost, which adds three to five dB of high-end enhancement, improving clarity of speech and adding definition to instrument sounds.

I really like this on acoustic guitars, placing it between the sound whole and the fifth fret, angled a bit toward the body. Like many other microphones we've discussed, the 1000 S is great when used in conjunction with another mic, for instance, when adding a 414 over the right shoulder of the player to capture the room sound of the guitar and blending it in with the 1000 S.

Figure 4.13 LR Baggs Microphone System with an actual live mic in the body of the guitar with blend controls
Erik Christian Photography

LR Baggs Microphone System

Leo Kottke used the first LR Baggs product, the LB6 Series Pickup. The octave Acoustic Guitar Pickup System combines an all-discrete, Class A FET pre-amp built on a stereo strap jack. It is assisted by an internal mic that is connected underneath the guitar top. The pre-amp also features a second octave input, so you can easily run a second pickup to complement the LR Baggs. It is an incredible system and completely preserves the integrity of the acoustic tone. I usually plug directly into the Universal Audio 610 mic pre-amp and record. With its various contour controls, plus the EQ control on the 610, the Baggs makes getting the right tone a breeze. Combine this system with any of the mics already discussed, such as the 414 or the TLM 49, and you'll get an extremely full sound. Also, try panning the Baggs to the right and the TLM 49 to the left and placing the 414 straight up at twelve o'clock in the mix.

Figure 4.14 A pair of Shure Stereo KSM137 microphones used for overheads on drums
Erik Christian Photography

Shure KSM137 Stereo Microphones

I've used these in stereo to record drum overheads and piano. It
is a condenser microphone with a cardioid polar pattern and can
withstand very high sound pressure levels. It has an extended frequency response, making it ideal for recording drum overheads and
hi-hats. Also there is a three-position low-frequency filter to limit
unwanted noise and proximity effect. It can capture sounds between
twenty Hz and twenty thousand Hz, which is optimal in recording
drums. You can accidently drop them and abuse them with no wor-
ries, because they are pretty much bullet proof, perfect for the home
recording application.

Figure 4.15 AKG C418 clip-on drum
microphone
Erik Christian Photography

AKG C418

This is a miniature condenser clip-on microphone specifically made for percussion frequencies. I've had great results with these on the snare drums where it is so tight to get a mike stand in, or in live applications. These are also great used in conjunction with a microphone like a Shure 57 miking the bottom of the snare. You can blend the two mics on the mixer with the faders and get a nice tone. Since it has a hypercardioid polar pattern, it rejects leakage from nearby instruments, so you can mic an entire band live and still get drum isolation.

Figure 4.16 Tools of the trade: the many different microphone adapters
Erik Christian Photography

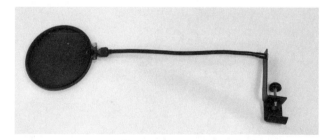

Figure 4.17 Wind screen, a necessity when recording vocals
Erik Christian Photography

GETTING MONSTER GUITAR TONE

Figure 4.18 Marshall Plexi head modified for sheer sustain and balls!
Erik Christian Photography

Achieving great guitar tone is like chasing after the "Holy Grail"—the search is endless. We are constantly trying to find the right balance between our human hands, strings, wood, amps, and pedals to get that "archangel of tone." You know it when you hear it. Whether it is the sweet, clean sound of George Benson's L-5 from *The Other Side of Abbey Road*, Johnny Marr's melodic voicing under Morrissey's vocals in The Smiths, or the sheer earth-shattering tone from Van Halen's "Eruption," it moves you, inspires you, and even pisses you off! That's guitar tone!

I've been very fortunate to have produced and recorded some of the greatest guitarists on the *Guitar Master Series* for BHP MUSIC. The series contained rarity tracks like "54-46 Was My Number" by Toots and the Maytals that featured Jeff Beck, and the track "B Fingers" by John Paul Jones from Led Zeppelin. I then started composing songs for top-notch shredders to add to the guitar compilations. I would produce and engineer the songs, play the guitar melodies, and then have each guest play the harmonies and we would both trade solos.

The one thing I love about guitar is that you just can't fake it. You've got to be able to play. I found that the tone really comes from the fingers; of course, all of the other parts matter, but a great guitarist can make a crappy guitar sound good.

During his first tour in the late '70s, Eddie Van Halen would let other guitarists from accompanying tour bands play his guitar through his whole rig, yet he noticed that none of the players could sound like him. They couldn't match his sound, so there's a lot to be said about the human touch.

Figure 4.19 Marshall four-by-twelve cabinet miked by Royer 101
Erik Christian Photography

The basics

Guitar tone can be dependent on your amp and the effects you place in the chain between you and the amp. A vintage Fender Super Reverb, played at lower levels, has a nice clarity, but as you raise the volume you get a sweet bite as the four- by ten-inch speakers start to break up.

Bear in mind, it will also depend on the axe you choose. For example, a Strat will have an entirely different tone from a Les Paul Custom, but this is a good, clean palette to start with. Now to get some overdrive, you can choose a plethora of pedals, but let's take an original Ibanez Tube Screamer 808 or an MXR Distortion Plus. Well hell, there you have it—a tone set up for a king.

Pedals can play an important part of the guitar tone, but I think one has to be careful not to get overly enthusiastic about pedals, resulting in the over-effected sounds that came out of the '80s hair band days. Choose subtle pedals—they will not alter your inherent guitar tone, but enhance it. Nevertheless, there is a time when an effect is called for, such as the classic Electro-Harmonix Memory Man, for instance. I've used it for many extreme sound effects in particular songs; in fact, even non-guitar bands have used it for color. The Chemical Brothers used it all over their breakthrough record, *Dig Your Own Hole*.

Figure 4.20 Marshall 4x12 cabinet miked by Beyerdynamic M160, best damn ribbon—good enough for Hendrix, it should be good enough for you!
Erik Christian Photography

Figure 4.21 Ampeg Bass Mini Classic Stack
miked with the Electro Voice RE20
Erik Christian Photography

Hammer of the Gods

Through my guitar tone journey since childhood, I've always been intrigued with what makes players choose their weapons of choice. So I've asked some of these inspiring players to share their setups:

Steve Morse: "I start with my normal Musicman electric, and then used a Buscarino acoustic/electric nylon string guitar, an Ovation steel string, a Steinberger 12-string, a Musicman baritone guitar (tuned down to B) and a Line 6. For amps, I'm enjoying the new signature amp that ENGL made for me, and a stock ENGL classic tube amp."

Eric Johnson: "My typical setup is a BK Butler Tube Driver or an AC Booster through a Marshall JMP Super Lead and a Dunlop Dallas Arbiter Fuzz Face or an old Ibanez Tube Screamer through a Marshall JTM 45. Then I have some that are more super lead JMP that have a lot of gain within the amp. I also have a twin reverb that has eminence speakers in it and when you crank it up it has an interesting type of lead tone."

Joe Satriani: "I plug my JS1000 guitar into various pedals, and/or go into a variety of amps heads, then on to a Palmer speaker simulator. Sometimes a plug-in would do the trick, or just all the pedals we found on the floor plugged in and turned up! We had much success with the Mooger Fooger pedals, the Fulltone Ultimate Octave, a Digitech Whammy pedal, and a pre-amp called a Hafler Triple Giant. The latter had the most robotic distortion, totally devoid of warmth and feeling. But, in the context of a song like 'Borg Sex,' it was perfect!"

Steve Vai: "EQ plays a vital role. I always keep a pair of C14s and a pair of 414s (mics) spread apart in the corners of the room. This is mixed into the sound at various levels depending on the desired effect. It's important to me to try and create a space for each guitar; the song should tell you what to do. I usually use Wave and Renaissance plug-ins for EQ, then compress analog before it hits the drive. I'm not a fan of digital compressors or reverbs."

Billy Sheehan: "I have an Ampeg SVT (turned way down!), as well as an Avalon pre-amp for direct sound. I use my regular bass that I play on stage, the Yamaha Attitude with RotoSound strings. We miked up the SVT cab, as well as split signals for a direct through a Radial Engineering direct box."

As the saying goes, "It's not just the destination, but the journey—and what you've experienced through the journey." This can easily be applied to your journey to great guitar tone. Sometimes, I find myself going back to the basics, with no pedals or effects; I plug my Les Paul in a well-made Marshall half-stack and just go for it. As Zappa said, "Shut Up 'n Play Yer Guitar!"

RECORDING LIVE INSTRUMENTS

There are three important stages to recording instruments in the studio: the instrument, the microphone, and the mic pre-amp. If one is not good, then all of it falls apart. The thing about recording is getting the desired sound you initially hear in the room. So if you are not recording the desired tone, the easiest thing to do is move the microphone placement. Some engineers may just use EQ to achieve their tone, but I don't like to commit any effects or EQ to print. I can always do that later in the mix, so I try to get the most natural unaffected tone in the room when I record. This is why I'm partial to ribbon mics; they seem to get the natural tone of the instrument with no harsh coloration.

When recording, there are other tangibles to consider, like whether you will be using twenty-four-track analog, two-track analog, or digital multi-track. For instance, today we assume that most people at home will be recording to some sort of digital application on their computer. In that case it is desirable to have a tube mic pre or tube mic to warm up the signal, because digital can have a real cold tone at times. Sure you can get plug-ins to distort the sound here and there, but the best recordings are always from a good initial source. Believe it or not, I still record to an Otari MTR 90 twenty-four-track, two-inch analog tape machine. Yes that's right, because no damn plug-in on the market will ever emulate it or give that wonderful tape saturation to acoustic drums! I use the best of both worlds and once I'm done with everything I need to get onto tape, I'll transfer it to Pro Tools to edit, or fly parts into the session. Even in Pro Tools, all of the tracks run through my Trident console so I can use all of my outboard rack gear and the Trident's EQs and effects sends. I have an old Digi 002 link to a Focusrite Octopre that were both upgraded and modified by Black Lion Audio. I have to say it sounds just as good if not better than Pro Tools HD at a fraction of the cost. Something to think about for those of you who have various interfaces, go to their site, http://blacklionaudio.com, and see what they can offer your units. I heard a distinct difference when I received the Digi 002; they upgraded the power supply, AD and DA converters, upgraded the master clock, the analog stage, and the pre-amps as well.

Figure 4.22 Otari MTR 90 twenty-four-track, two-inch machine in action—smell the tape!
Erik Christian Photography

Figure 4.22 Otari MTR 90 Remote—ahh, so much easier to record than using a mouse!
Erik Christian Photography

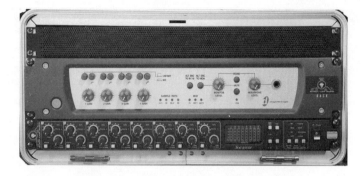

Figure 4.24 Digi 002 and Focusrite Octopre, both tweaked out and modified by Black Lion Audio, better than HD!
Erik Christian Photography

Horns

Remember when recording instruments to set the microphone gain down to the lowest point when you are first getting sounds, because a horn player can easily blow out your mic and monitors. I always place the switch on my AKG 414 to negative 20 dB when recording saxophones or trumpets because they inevitably will pin all of my meters. Also make sure they stand back at least five inches from the mic. But with that being said, I always see them move closer and closer to the mic, as we get further into the song, until the microphone is in the bell. Horn players have this innate ability to move all around the room, they never seem to stand in one place too long, so it's always good to give them a little headroom when recording.

Figure 4.25 Trumpet with the Voodoo VR1
Erik Christian Photography

Figure 4.26 Saxophone
miked with the sE ribbon
tube microphone
Erik Christian Photography

You also can use one microphone for a small horn section to capture horn hits, which will capture the ambience of the room as well. The only downside to this technique is that you are committed to all of the horn levels, meaning you can't go back when mixing and make one horn louder than the other on the track. If there are solos involved, I usually get all of the horn hits done, and then record solos on separate tracks so I have control in the mix to place effects and dynamics on each track. Depending on the song, I usually compress horns after it is printed.

Figure 4.27 Saxophone
miked with AKG 414 captures
a great tone
Erik Christian Photography

Drums and percussion

There are so many ways to mic drums—the minimal approach, close miking every drum, or multi miking everything on the floor. I like the close mic approach, but usually I use one microphone on each drum. By doing so I make sure I get all of the drum sounds correct before recording. That's why it's always good to get the drummer to the session a couple of hours before everyone else gets to the studio. Nothing worse than trying to get drum sounds when the bass player is telling jokes in the control room and the horn players are screeching out notes. You have to be careful because drummers will start moving mikes once the session starts. Man, I had this one drummer in a session that decided to completely move the 57 and the stand off of the snare; I mean like four feet off. Thank God I caught it early on and put it back. And this was after taking an hour to get the drum sounds right. Everyone in the room was like why did you move the mic and he said in his Brooklyn accent, "Ah cause it dwas in my way!" That's why I like the mini clip AKG mics for the snare, so they can't move it and it won't be in their way. Be sure to always check the mics on the drums after every take to make sure they haven't been bumped into or moved by accident. (Hey did you hear about the guitar player that got away with parking in a handicap spot? He put drumsticks on the dash. Or what did the drummer say to the bandleader? Do you want me to play too fast or too slow?) Just joking, some of my best friends are drummers.

Figure 4.28 Snare close miked with a Shure SM 57
Erik Christian Photography

Figure 4.29 AKG C418 clip microphone on snare
Erik Christian Photography

Usually I like to mic rack toms with a Sennheiser 421 and floor toms with an Electro Voice RE20, the kick with an AKG D112, and a snare with a 57. Now with overheads, I like AKG 414s and notice that the larger diaphragm captures the body tone of the toms as well. I have never liked the way drums sound recorded directly to Pro Tools, Logic, or any other DAW out there. So I print to two-inch tape along with the bass guitar and rhythm guitars. The tape fattens up the drum tones and adds a very nice quality of saturation tone. Recording to digital sounds so thin and cold and doesn't have the dimensions that we've come to expect from record quality music. I also like to use a mono room mic like the Neumann TLM 49. I put it through a 1176 compressor with "all buttons in" to compress the crap out of it and print it to a separate track. I can bring it in the mix with a fader to give dimension to the drum kit. In the drum room I use a portable twenty-five-foot-long, eight-channel XLR box to get the close miking done, and on the other end I have TT male connectors that plug right into my Trident patch bay that are normalled to the mic pres on the desk. It is very convenient and efficient to make the work flow easy and quick.

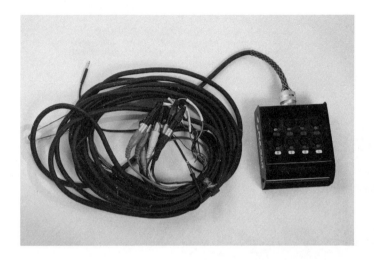

Figure 4.30 Portable XLR box with twenty-five-foot snake with TT male adaptors
Erik Christian Photography

Figure 4.31 AKG D112 microphone dead on the kick beater
Erik Christian Photography

Figure 4.32 Electro Voice RE20 on floor tom
Erik Christian Photography

Figure 4.33 Sennheiser 421 on rack tom
Erik Christian Photography

Figure 4.34 Sennheiser 421 on floor tom
Erik Christian Photography

Figure 4.35 Shure Stereo pair of KSM137 miking drums as overheads
Erik Christian Photography

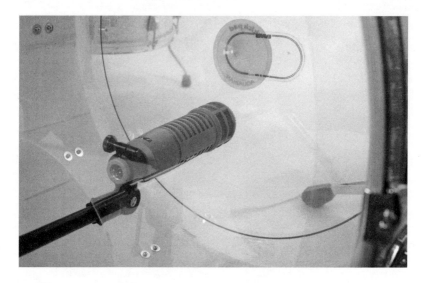

Figure 4.36 Electro Voice RE20 miking the kick drum
Erik Christian Photography

Figure 4.37 Shure SM 57 underneath snare and AKG C418 clip-on mic
Erik Christian Photography

Figure 4.38 Neumann TLM 49 used in front of drum set as room mic with the Electro Voice RE20 inside kick drum
Erik Christian Photography

As for percussion instruments, there are a variety of microphones you can use. I've used AKG 414s, ribbon mics, sE RN17 Stereo Pair designed by Rupert Neve, and larger capsule ones like the Neumann TLM 49. Because percussion instruments are so cutting, sometimes it's nice to use a tube pre-amp like the Universal Audio 610 to warm up the signal a bit as it goes into Pro Tools.

Figure 4.39 Neumann TLM 49 miking shaker
Erik Christian Photography

Figure 4.40 Neumann TLM 49 miking tambourine
Erik Christian Photography

Figure 4.41 Picture 39 djembe guiro
Erik Christian Photography

Figure 4.42 Neumann TLM 49
miking djembe
Erik Christian Photography

Chapter 5

Dynamic Processing

So what are dynamic processors and why should you know about them? Well, it is very important to your overall mix as well as to each individual track. For instance, with EQ you can make a bass track sound thinner or fatter depending on what frequencies you decide to attenuate or detonate. This holds true with compression, reverb, or any other processing you want to give to your tracks. This is the most important part of achieving a final mix, a snare with reverb, guitar with delay, a vocal with dimension and space. This is what separates a finished, polished mix from a home-recorded demo.

Below is a list of the most common signal processing:

- **Compression**

    Reducing the dynamic range while still letting the transient peaks pass through. Very useful, but remember, just because you have compressor plug-ins, it doesn't mean you have to use them on every single tack.

Figure 5.1 Tall rack full of analog outboard gear at Jungle Room Studios
Erik Christian Photography

- **Limiting**

  Slams the transient peaks while effecting the entire dynamic range. Careful though, you don't want to hear the track pump and breathe.

- **Chorus**

  Similar to a doubling effect, but regenerates the voice into a modulating sound. Not a big fan, so use it sparingly. In the '80s, it was so overused and sounded very over-processed.

- **Equalization**

  Three types—parametric, shelf and filter, and graphic—all let you adjust tonal qualities for various frequencies. Very abused. Instead, move the microphone before your EQ. Once Rupert Neve was told that his EQs were so popular that everyone used them, he replied, "I know. *That's* the problem."

- **Noise Gate**

  Exactly what it states, removes unwanted noise when the program is quiet. Think of a snare drum and all of the leakage of the drum kit around it, use a gate to get a clean snare hit and remove all of the hi-hat, cymbals, etc.

- **Reverberation**

  Simply determined by the size of the space you want to use on a track, room, hall, cathedral, etc. One of the things lacking in popular music today. Too bad because it can give a three-dimensional feel to instruments.

- **Pitch Shift**

  Can play a specific pitch from the original note, like a third or fifth up or down. Again another lost art in modern music, wonderfully inventive and fun to use.

- **Delay**

  This includes slapback, tape, multiple achieved by adjusting the rate, feedback and depth. Fantastic on guitar solos, trumpet, sax, and so many other lead instruments.

- **Flanging/Phaser**

  It is a delay that has a varied sweep effect from zero to twenty milliseconds creating a very filtered, sweeping sound. Listen to

Van Halen's *Unchained* or *And the Cradle Will Rock* . . . you'll hear it on the guitar riff. Another oldie but goodie that young engineers should rediscover.

- **Doubling**
  Used for an ambient effect to create a fatter track, usually a delay set between 15–35 milliseconds. It's usually the lazy man's way out of actually singing or playing the part again to create a true stereo effect. Note that some people use chorus to achieve the doubling effect.

When using any of these processing effects, keep in mind that a little goes a long way, so try not to overuse. I try never to use any of these effects when initially recording because you will be stuck with it forever. I'd rather have the flexibility of using these effects during the mix if necessary. I think there is a backlash from the years of using reverbs, delays, or flanging in popular music mixes. It seems that many of these mixes don't have much in terms of production value. There lacks dimension in the mixes or a sense of cohesiveness of the musicians playing together in the studio. Seems very sterile and thin sounding; maybe because everything is done on a laptop today, I can't put my finger on it really. Just like the resurgence of vinyl records in the past few years, there will be a point in the future where the next generation will realize that recording on analog tape really does sound better than recording in the box. Maybe it's all too easy now with simulation plug-ins, a million drum samples, guitar, keyboard, and vocal loops or simply the ability to create music without any prior knowledge of music. I remember there was this guy who wanted to be a composer, so I turned him onto the Stylus RMX years ago. He goes out and buys it and then tries to put these soundscapes with grooves together that sounded horrific, with no feeling or sense of composition and then asked me to add them to my catalog. Well of course, I let him down easy and told him that I didn't need new music at the moment. This was the same guy who wanted me to drag my Ampex MM1200 24 track analog machine to his studio thirty miles away so he wouldn't have to bring his drums to my recording studio! Really? Are you kidding, do you even have a clue how much the machine weighs? Hopeless, and to think that this guy wrote for a pro audio magazine was scary. OMG . . . this is what we have today!

Listen, I went to an audio engineering school many, many moons ago, and I think most of LA did as well. I worked as assistant engineer at Electric Lady Studios in NYC and was offered a job at The Hit Factory, but said no when I realized the duties included being a delivery boy. In my experience, the larger studios would never give an assistant a chance to do much, except clean the bathrooms and take their laundry to the cleaners. No thanks, man! I decided to work at smaller studios like Far & Away in New York and Powerhouse Studios in San Fernando Valley, California. In the smaller studios you were able to handle the equipment and engineer recordings during down times, something that rarely happened in the larger studios. But to be honest, it wasn't until I had my own studio and had to wire everything up myself, using it every day, that I truly understood signal flow and how the whole recording process worked from start to finish. It's like driving a car; you can read upside down and back and forth every book about the procedure of driving, but you won't know how to do it until you own a car and drive every day. This stands true with studio recording. I always used the engineering part as a vehicle for me as an artist. I went on to work at record companies like Restless Records and Virgin Records, learning all of the nuts and bolts of how the industry worked. Then I became a recording artist having been signed to different labels, then off to producing and opening up my own imprint, BHP Music, Ltd. In the '80s, it cost an unbelievable amount of money to buy equipment. A piece of crap Tascam or Fostex machine cost thousands of dollars, and then you would have to buy a mixer and outboard gear for thousands. Remember, back then there were no computers, plug-ins, not even ADATs or DA-88s. You were forced to record on analog gear. I wish we had some of these computers then, we could have been recording and producing even more stuff.

But for those of you who want to get a real handle on recording music, you should look to the past for techniques and combine them with modern methods. Deconstruct your favorite albums and see how they got those sounds and how they recorded them. If you like blues guitar tones, listen to your favorite blues artists and try to recreate the drum sounds, guitar, keyboard, etc. Maybe through this process you might discover an even better sound by experimenting with miking and placement. I know in today's world it's easier to just use some sort of ready-made virtual amp or drum loops, but really, that's not creating your own recordings. Just think of how many people are doing the very same thing.

Figure 5.2 Close-up of analog compressors/limiters at Jungle Room Studios
Erik Christian Photography

Now back to signal processors. If you are using a mixer of some type, analog or digital, you will be inserting the compressor, EQ, etc., in the signal chain by using the "send" and "return." If you are using some sort of effects processor hardware like a Harmonizer H3000, Lexicon PCM70, Eventide Eclipse, etc., you will set up your "aux sends" for that particular device and a stereo return to adjust your effects level. Now in the DAW this is achieved by choosing your inserts on each particular channel. It is interesting because you can define an era in the way recordings were produced. For example, in the '50s, slap echo and plate reverb were popular, whereas the '60s had the psychedelic sounds of the flange, wah wah, and fuzz tone. Then the late '70s and '80s utilized chorus, multi delays, and the huge gated snare tones. By the early '90s, drum machines had become the norm and the takeover of hip-hop had occurred. As the '90s marched on, more programmed drums and drum samples were commonplace with the DJ invasion. Through the 2000s, we saw the digital revolution explode where everyone bought a computer with some sort of recording program complete with a plethora of sounds. As technology has become more efficient with larger hard drives and faster processing power, we see our computers doing more for us. In 1990, whoever heard of a *terabyte?* Are you kidding, when we used samplers like the early Akai MPC series, four megabytes were considered a lot. So each era defines its own sound, limited to the technology available at the time. Just think what The Beatles could have done with today's technology.

COMPRESSORS/LIMITERS

Here is a list of useful hardware compressors/limiters that you may find intriguing to use on your next mix. There are quite a lot out there and this is just a small sample, so the best way is to test them. Many of the manufacturers are willing for people to demo their equipment, especially newer, small companies that are trying to get their product out in the market.

Electro-Harmonix NY-2A Stereo Limiter

Figure 5.3 Electro Harmonix Super Optical Compressor NY-2A
Erik Christian Photography

What kind of optical compressor can be so flexible that it allows the user to adjust the actual light source from incandescent, to LED, to electroluminescent with a rotary knob? Welcome to the world of the NY-2A Limiter by Electro-Harmonix. The incandescent lamp has the slowest attack time, with a little kink in its response. The LED lamp has a much faster attack time and a much faster frequency response. The electroluminescent (EL) lamp has the most interesting reaction to frequencies; it actually changes colors with each frequency range. So the EL lamp produces less light at low frequencies, more in the middle, and much more at high frequencies. There is also a squash switch that will act as high-frequency shelving for the EL lamp. How does it sound? Fantastic for guitars! You can do a lot of experimenting with the unit on different guitar parts, with the flexibility of the settings. Again the controls are very simple, with Pre-Gain, Compress, and Post-Gain knobs, so a lot of the compression will depend on your input level.

Rupert Neve 5043 Compressor-Limiter

Figure 5.4 Rupert Neve 5043 Dual Compressor Portico Series
Erik Christian Photography

This is a fantastic stereo bus compressor, which can also be used as two independent compressor-limiters (channels A and B). This type of compressor technology uses a VCA, or voltage-controlled amplifier. There are many types of voltage controls, including the use of tubes, discrete and integrated solid-state circuits, and naturally nonlinear devices, each one having its own sonic character. This has a very accurate low-noise, low-distortion VCA: in other words, very transparent. But with that said, it does have that Neve sound without being too obtrusive. Great for rock music of all types, it has such a beautiful full sound that really makes the guitar pop out of the track. It also can add a gain from negative six dB to twenty dB and has a ratio from 1:1 all the way to 40:1. This compressor is so musical and loves guitars of all sorts. I used this quite a lot on producing the *Guitar Masters, Volume 3 & 4: Les Paul Dedication*, everything from bass to stereo bus compressor from the mix to crunch guitars. This is also very good across the mix bus.

Trident Dual Limiter-Compressor CB9146

Figure 5.5 Trident Dual Limiter-Compressor CB9146
Erik Christian Photography

This is probably one of the most transparent compressors I've ever used. I don't want a compressor to stamp a color or sound onto my guitars. I just want to control uneven levels and retain the natural tone of the guitar. As with the 1176, this uses the FET technology, and it's very easy to use with the color-coded knobs. However, the Trident has attack and release controls, which the 1176 lacks. In fact, the Trident has a large variety of control combinations that can achieve different compression. It is great on a bus as well as for drums or guitars, leaving the natural characteristics of the source tone. These are real classic limiters dating back to the '70s. In fact, you couldn't get breathing effect if you tried. This compressor is so musical and highly recommended.

Universal Audio 1176

Figure 5.6 Universal Audio 1176n Limiter
Erik Christian Photography

Figure 5.7 Universal Audio Dual 1176, you can never have enough!
Erik Christian Photography

Technically, this is a gain-limiting amplifier using the FET technology. So what's an FET? The acronym stands for "field effect transistor," which is used as a voltage-controlled variable resistor shunt. Using the FET enables large amounts of limiting without getting increased distortion. In other words, the stuff sounds good! It's very easy to use, by controlling the input; you are controlling the compression along with the compression ratio from 4:1 to 20:1. It sounds fantastic on so many things, from acoustic guitars to bass guitars and even percussions, such as a snare drum.

When producing bass virtuoso on Randy Coven's CD, *Nu School*, I used this on his bass all the time, because it reacted well to his tone and style of playing, on both the five-string and piccolo bass. It also worked perfectly when used on a mono drum room mic with all of the buttons in. It gave that huge, over-compressed sound. I would blend the track into the drum mix to give some ambience.

Urei LA-4

Figure 5.8 Vintage pair of Urei LA-4 Compressor/Limiters
Erik Christian Photography

One of my all-time favorites is the optical Limiter Urei LA-4, probably one of the best compressors for the guitar. It is extremely transparent, very easy to use, and very flexible. The difference between the LA-4 and its predecessor, the LA-3A, is the added ratio control, without the added confusion of attack and release controls introduced on newer optical limiters. Any tech will tell you that the whole beauty of Optos in general is their simplicity. In fact, it shines on just about any stringed instrument, whether bass, acoustic guitar, electric guitars, even Rhodes and the organ. The best trait of this limiter is that it is actually difficult to make it sound bad. I have a pair that I had recapped (capacitors replaced), and the quality of sound that it produces on a lead guitar and solo is mind-blowing. It handles the guitar signal flawlessly, without losing the tone or dynamics. This is something of utmost importance: you don't want to disturb the tone you worked so hard to get recorded! I generally use it on various guitars during a mix to control everything at the final stage.

Purple Audio MC77

Figure 5.9 Purple Audio MC77 Compressor/Limiter
Erik Christian Photography

Do you like the classic FET sound of the Urei 1176? Well, think of the MC77 as an 1176 on steroids. This bad purple monster kicks some serious booty! It has the identical controls of the 1176 but a fatter squash. Just like the 1176, the front panel has two large knobs, two small knobs, a meter, and two columns of buttons. The large knobs adjust input and output levels; the small knobs adjust attack and release times. And yes, it has the all-buttons capability to really get that crush for drums. In fact, when I record drums, I put a mono room mic through it and push all the buttons in to get a pseudo Bonham sound. But I love using it on guitar, especially crunchy rhythm guitar to give it some girth. It also shines on bass, giving it some presence in a mix, without the muddy effect.

I usually track using the MC77 on rhythm acoustic guitar to control the transients, while bringing out the attack of the pick on the strings. This is a bit more colored-sounding than the LA-4, but used in the right way, it has wonderful results in a mix.

Anthony DeMaria 1500

Figure 5.10 Anthony DeMaria 1500 Stereo Tube Compressor
Erik Christian Photography

The brilliance of Mr. DeMaria comes all out in this fantastic-sounding limiter. Similar to the LA-4, the 1500 utilizes Opto attenuators to create "invisible" compression. It's a two-channel, all-tube design with phenomenal dynamic range. It boasts eight vacuum tubes, giving it unmistakable richness and depth. This unit has an incredible cross-platform use, from being a beefy bus compressor to limiting individual instruments. I love using this on guitars; the tubes add fullness without coloring the signal. On acoustic guitars . . . *forgettaboutit*! It makes them stand out with a creaminess of tube circuitry.

I usually route two rhythm guitar tracks through it in stereo to achieve a warm presence in the mix. The only thing you have to be mindful of is your headroom; you can't push it like the 1176 without getting undesirable distortion. So for those of you who record directly in a DAW with amp modeling plug-ins, this would be the ideal compressor for you to have at mix down, to warm up that cold digital signal.

Anthony DeMaria 670

This is the Rolls-Royce of limiters; some may call it the Holy Grail of compression. It is a reproduction of the classic Fairchild 670. It is truly a sonic beast and sounds unbelievable. On guitars, it adds such an incredible punch and clarity delivered from the eighteen tubes and fourteen transformers, really putting the "F" in *fat*! It's handmade like a tank with "military strength"; every detail has been scrutinized to perfection to re-create the original. Surprisingly easy to use, it has four control knobs, input gain, ratio, DC threshold, and a fine-tune threshold. These last two controls are interactive with each other, which is a fantastic idea. You can set your threshold point and then use the fine-tune knob to dial in a compression point you are seeking. The saying "a little goes a long way" is very true when using the ADL 670 on guitars. You don't need to see the VU meters moving about to get the compression effect. On rhythm guitar the limiter gives a punch, especially if you have a real crunch tone. But the great thing about this limiter is that it delivers a velvety smooth sound that creates fullness in the track for guitar.

Overall, I believe the trick to understanding compression and how it works is experimenting with different compressors on guitar and seeing how they interact with the track. Some compressors just don't do it for a guitar track, no matter how hard you try. Keep in mind that compressors are designed to keep the dynamics under control in a track, so be very careful not to overuse it on guitars, or you'll hear the pumping, or what is known as "breathing," of the guitar, which means you should back off the compressor.

The most important factor for me when choosing a compressor for a guitar is how it will enhance the guitar without coloration to the tone. There are some guitar tracks you may never need to compress, such as a high-gain lead tone. The tubes of the amp have already done the compression, and the higher the gain, the less dynamics, because the pre-amp gain stage in the amp is doing just that: compressing the guitar tone with the gain sound. Be careful to always monitor the VU meter during gain reduction as well, because it is very easy to overdo it. Generally, negative three dB is a safe place to be. Use your ears, and you will be fine.

Figure 5.11 AMS-Neve 33609c Stereo Compressor-Limiter
Erik Christian Photography

This is considered to be the desert island compressor by many. I love it across the mix bus; in fact, that's what I designate it to be in the studio, strictly a bus compressor. It has a fat, warm tone and will thicken even the thinnest mixes. It is still built to its original 1970s specifications from Rupert Neve. It has hand-wired transformers and gain reduction circuitry that produces a very smooth signal even at extreme settings. It utilizes a discrete output stage like the original model, for a slightly warmer sound. The compressor and limiter have separate sections, with independent threshold, recovery, and attack controls. The compressor section offers ratios from 1.5:1 to 6:1 with gain make-up controls.

JDK R-22 Dual Compressor

Figure 5.12 JDK R-22 Stereo Compressor-Limiter
Erik Christian Photography

This is a real powerhouse, fantastic on drum overheads. In fact, I used it on all of the drum overheads on producing/engineering *Guitars for Wounded Warriors*, featuring Steve Morse, Billy Sheehan, Reb Beach (Whitesnake), Bumblefoot (Guns N' Roses), Gary Hoey, Hal Lindes (Dire Straits), Alex De Rosso (Dokken), and Chuck Loeb. Also great on guitars, it really gives that extreme compression sound on rock rhythm riffs. It has the patented API feature of the *Thrust* circuit, which slams your mix. This is the same compressor circuit originally designed into all ATI Paragon mixing consoles. The two channels can even be linked for use as a stereo compressor with true RMS power summing of the left and right signals.

Manley Elop Electro-Optical Limiter, dual-channel

Figure 5.13 Manley Elop Electro-Optical Limiter, dual-channel
Erik Christian Photography

Wonderfully smooth and warm-sounding compressor. I've used it in so many applications, from compressing horns to overheads and across the mix buss. It's super easy to operate, which spawns the term "set it and forget it." It operates on the principle of audio signal to shine an LED (Light Emitting Diode) onto an LDR (Light Dependent Resistor). This is the same technology that Teletronix & Urei used on their LA-2A, LA-3, and LA-4 limiters. These units used a slower electro-luminescent panel-light on a conventional LDR encased in a light-tight enclosure. The Elop consists of Class A amps where the audio signal passes through Manley tubes technology. The end result is a very clean limiter that can be used in stereo or on two individual instruments.

DBX Quad Compressor 1046

Figure 5.14 DBX Quad Compressor 1046
Erik Christian Photography

You can simply never have enough hardware compressors in a studio! Having four in one rack space is that much better. I use this on toms or rhythm guitars once I run out of all of my other compressors.

Each channel consists of Threshold, OverEasy (characteristics of the original dbx 160), Ratio, Input/Output Meter, Output Gain, Bypass, PeakStopPlus (allows you to set the maximum signal level you want to pass through this channel), and Stereo Link (allows you to link channels one and two, and three and four, for two channels of true stereo compression). This is a perfect solution for the home recording guys because to get four compressors in one rack, for the price you can't beat it.

EQ

JDK R24 Dual Channel 4-Band EQ

Figure 5.15 JDK R24 Dual Channel EQ
Erik Christian Photography

This is a great, flexible EQ that has an array of applications for recording. You can warm up a guitar sound or notch out certain frequencies with ease. This was modeled after the classic APSI model 562 EQ, and each band offers continuously variable control of frequency and gain, using separate knobs. It has twelve dB of boost/cut per band, and all four bands are peak/dipping parametric configuration with a high headroom plus twenty-four dB clip level. The great thing is that this EQ has a very transparent sound, which is perfect for guitar tracks, so the original guitar tone is not altered. You can even put it across a mix buss because they come in pairs. I put it across a guitar stereo mix, and once I placed it into the whole mix, the guitars popped right out of the speakers. Remember that with EQ, a little goes a long way, so experiment all you want before the final mix.

Pulse Techniques EQP-1A3

Figure 5.16 Pulse Techniques EQP-1A3 Program EQ
Erik Christian Photography

The Pulse EQP-1A3 sounds fantastic. I put a couple of mono guitar tracks through it and put it to the test. First, I ran an aggressive bass part by Billy Sheehan, and I have to say it really gave it a full spectrum of sound, without the mud. It let me hone into the low-mids, which gave the bass true detail, as well as sharpened up the notes in the mix. On Billy's solo part, it worked beautifully by letting me attenuate the higher mid frequencies to showcase his solo.

I also put a Frank Gambale solo I recorded through the EQP-1A3 with pleasing results. The tubes really gave warmth to the aggressively distorted guitar tone, without taking away from their signature sounds. Having the bandwidth from sharp to broad is a great asset to carve in the sound. I found myself not even looking at the unit, but just slowly dialing in the tone with my head between the monitors, stopping when I hit the mark! The ears don't lie, and the EQP-1A3 is a great tool for those who still believe that sound matters.

Trident Parametric EQ CB9066

Figure 5.17 Trident Parametric EQ CB9066
Erik Christian Photography

This is my go-to EQ for guitars and bass. It is probably the most transparent parametric EQ I have ever heard. Like all of the classic Trident gear, the Parametric EQ consists of five color-coded section knobs. The blue knob controls the frequency (100 Hz to 400 Hz) and slope (zero dB to twenty-two dB); the gold knobs are the bandwidth pot, dB gain (negative sixteen to positive sixteen), and frequency pot (60 Hz to 700 Hz); the black knobs control bandwidth pot, dB gain (negative sixteen to positive sixteen) and frequency pot (600 Hz to seven kHz); the red knobs control the bandwidth pot, dB gain (negative sixteen to positive sixteen), and frequency pot (three and a half kHz to fourteen Kz); and the green knobs control frequency (four kHz to fifteen kHz) and slope (zero dB to twenty-two dB).

Rupert Neve Portico 5033 5-Band EQ

Figure 5.18 Rupert Neve 5033 EQ Portico Series
Erik Christian Photography

I want to preface the following with the comment that there's no magic box; if there were, everybody would have bought one years ago, and there would be no need for any other device. Rupert Neve once said, "The problem with my EQs is that everyone uses them"—the point being that it is traditionally thought that EQ is seldom used, and if there is need for EQ on a source, you should move the microphone and re-record the source instead of using EQ at all.

With that said, Neve EQs do rock, and the 5033 is no exception! The input and output transformers are custom designed by Neve, which is the real secret to all Neves. The EQ is based on his traditional curves, negative/positive twelve dB input level adjustment, and it has that Neve sound; it's not as transparent as other EQs, but it still has the Neve hallmark sound. It is an incredibly flexible EQ, and you can really dial a plethora of sounds from corrective EQ or use it as an effect.

Orban Parametric EQ Model 622B

Figure 5.19 Orban Dual Parametric EQ Model 622B
Erik Christian Photography

This is an awesome tool to have in your recording arsenal. It is a dual EQ that offers four bands, each with tuning and bandwidth control, true parametric operation: non-interacting control over all these equalization parameters, positive sixteen dB to infinity equalization range, "Constant-Q" curves, each band tuning over 25:1 frequency range, and "Q" a variable between 0.29 and 3.2.

So what does that mean? It means that it is one heck of an EQ. Originally these were designed for broadcast use, but they quickly became a studio favorite. I frequently use the 622B on drums and when I want to dial in the heavy guitar rhythm *a la* Pantera or Megadeth territory. The filters are well made, and notch filtering is achieved easily. By adjusting the MLF and MHF bands close together in frequency, you can achieve that old telephone or radio effect. You can also get the amp hum off of a track by using the narrowband-notching mode, which is very helpful when using those single coils or P90s in the studio.

Akai MFC42 Analog Filter Module

Figure 5.20 AKAI Analog Filter MFC42
Erik Christian Photography

I really enjoy working with this unit. I put some overdriven guitars through it for an electronic TV score I was working on for ABC-TV. The EQ features a stereo and a mono filter channel, which can be controlled independently, linked together, or inverted. Each channel is selectable between any one of four filter types: low pass, high pass, band pass, and notch. The stereo channel features dual two-pole or four-pole filters, and the mono channel has two-pole, four-pole, or eight-pole selectable filters (maximum combination is four two-pole filters total).

The effects are dynamite: distortion with depth control, analog stereo phase shifter with speed and depth controls, and master EQ with separate low and high controls. These controls make it easy to get those sweeping filter effects on guitar tracks. What is extremely cool is that you can control the movement of each knob or button via MIDI recording to an external sequencer for complete automation. I used this quite a lot on the Asphalt Jungle recordings to get those huge filter sweeps on guitars.

Pulse Techniques MEQ-5

Figure 5.21 Pulse Techniques MEQ-5 Mid-Range EQ
Erik Christian Photography

I can't say enough great things about this tube EQ, very musical and underrated. In his typical fashion, Steve Jackson has made a faithful rec-reation of the original Pultec mid-range EQ. It brings all of the detail out of the material. Crisp midrange can shine through on snares and guitars in a mix with this EQ. The MEQ-5 gives you two bands of boost and attenu-ation bands to shape and carve your tone. Everything between 200Hz and 7kHz can be affected by the MEQ-5 giving the ability to hone in specific frequencies. The great thing is that it is not an over-the-top EQ, but rather a very subtle one, which is why it is so musical. Plus the fact that buying an original Pultec EQ carries a hefty price, the Pulse makes them exact to spec and with modern components with similar results.

USEFUL GEAR

BAE 1073 Microphone Pre-amp

Figure 5.22 aBAE 1073 Microphone Pre-amp
Erik Christian Photography

This is a sweet-sounding mic pre based on the classic Neve 1073. It uses the same 283 card and transformers as the original for a fraction of the cost. For those of you who are doing digital recording only, this is a must-have mic pre for guitar! It adds warmth to the guitar tone and fattens up the overall sound. It has a very present tone, so you really hear the attack of the pick and fingers on the fretboard without having to compress. It adds sub harmonics to the bottom end, making it feel large without the mud, and it adds silkiness to the high frequencies, giving it a sheen. It has a red gain knob and a gray output. Every click on the gain knob is a 5-dB increment, so you can always adjust the output level to get in between the five dB steps. With its large headroom, it is an excellent choice for the low-output ribbon microphones.

JDK R20 Microphone Pre-amp

Figure 5.23 JDK R20 Microphone Pre-amp
Erik Christian Photography

It's great having a mic pre-amp with VU meters for monitoring output/input levels. This is a very well-made mic pre. And how can you go wrong with the design team of API behind it? With the pad switch attenuating the microphone signal by twenty dB (the instrument signal by ten dB) and the fifty-four dB of gain, this is a good choice for most microphones. Though some would say it's not enough gain for a ribbon mic, I've never had a problem miking a cabinet. It has a nice warm, transparent sound that leaves the precious guitar tone intact.

Extremely easy to use with two gain knobs that determine your input/output signals, it has a smooth sound that captures the accurate guitar tone as you hear it in the room. This is a very different type of mic pre from the BAE 1073 because it is a transformerless mic pre-amp, which means the gain stage is directly wired as opposed to running through a transformer, common in classic mic pres. It's very affordable and a fine choice for all types of guitars.

DBX 1074 Quad Noise Gate

Figure 5.24 DBX 1074 Quad Noise Gate
Erik Christian Photography

Like the DBX 1046 compressor, this is a quad noise gate; very reliable and necessary in any studio for recording live instruments. I use these on kick, snare, and toms on a live-recorded drum set. I usually don't gate when recording, only after, during the mix. Each channel has an independent threshold and release control, independent key filtering, and connects by a balanced gold-plated XLR or quarter-inch inputs and outputs. Again, with the price point and what you get, this is ideal for the home recordist.

Urei Platform

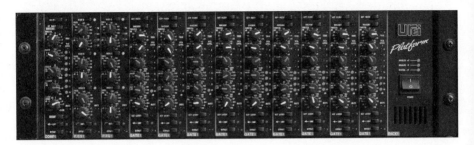

Figure 5.25 Urei Platform Pre has been the lunchbox craze in recent years!
Erik Christian Photography

In the early '90s, the Urei Platform was made in Denmark, which was the predecessor to the lunchboxes of today like the API 500 series. Made to last and sounding great, these were racks that could be interchanged with one of four modules: Compressor, Parametric EQ, Noise Gate, or Mic Pre-amp. This is my go-to rack for gating drums, very accurate and you can really dial in the sound. You can still find these on eBay or Craigslist today at an affordable price. I have a parametric EQ module and a compressor that I use on snare that sound fantastic. I have never seen a plug-in that imitates this yet!

Alesis Masterlink

Figure 5.26 Alesis Masterlink High Resolution Master Disk Recorder
Erik Christian Photography

This is a great option if you are mixing through a physical mixer, because you can use all of your racks of hardware while you warm up your Pro Tools signal, but still mix it down to a hard drive. You can set the recording resolution up to twenty-four-bit, ninety-six kHz, and forty gigs of internal memory. It burns standard Red Book CDs at sixteen-bit, 44.1kHz and will burn a CD24 for high-resolution files. There is also an editing feature and mastering tool enabling parametric EQ, compression, limiting, and normalizing. You can organize songs in playlists doing fade-ins, fade-outs, track gain, start points, track cropping, and store sixteen different playlists containing up to ninety-nine songs per list. If you are not stuck in the box, this is a very good thing to mix down to, especially if you are creating fast projects for television and film. I'm on my second Masterlink now. The only thing is that I wish they had installed a USB port so you could have the option of downloading files to a computer.

Chapter 6

Mix

Figure 6.1 Custom Trident Trimix 32 Channel 16 Bus
Erik Christian Photography

The proof is in the pudding, as they say! This is the most important step. A great recording mixed badly doesn't make a bit of difference, if it does not sound great altogether. Each individual track has to sit balanced properly with all of the others, or it doesn't amount to a hill of beans. It is very important to balance all of the instruments, as some say the best way to start is with a clean slate. I am always balancing tracks as I'm recording various instruments through the tracking stage, placing compressors on drums, guitars, effects on lead instruments, and so forth. This makes it much easier for my final mix because I have been living with the song for weeks/months and have been experimenting with tracks and how certain signal processors sound on particular instruments. Also, before you start mixing, look at your songs and see which ones you can keep together when mixing. For instance, if you are mixing three hard rock songs with drums, bass, guitars, and vocals, a piano ballad, and a electronic dance song, you are going to want to mix the hard rock songs one after the other, because the effects and processors you'll be using will be similar. Then you can move on to the piano ballad or the dance electronic song. It's called good workflow and it was very important when mixing through an analog mixer and using physical outboard gear through a patch bay. However, with the virtual mixers and computer recording of today, you can save all of your settings for each song session.

Figure 6.2 Custom Trident Trimix patch bay
Erik Christian Photography

A piece of advice to take to heart is never play a rough mix for an idiot, especially an A&R guy, because he'll tell you it sounds like a rough mix, *duh!* When I was signed to Instinct records in the '90s, I went through this all the time. They would constantly tell me to send them demos of the song and then turn around and say, love the tunes, but they sound like demos. Well yeah, that's because they are demos and you said you wanted to hear how the song was coming along. The truth of the matter is never let anyone hear unfinished material because people say all sorts of stuff when they have no idea what they are talking about, especially A&R guys (not musicians) and marketing morons! Case in point, I remember when we were mixing my album in London for Instinct records called *Soft Touch*, and the producer sent a rough mix of the songs to the label in New York. We were all sitting in a room in London, having a conference call on speaker phone, when one of the genius A&R guys in NY asked, "What's that sound in the song that goes from side to side? It's very annoying." We figured out that the noise he was referring to was the suitcase Rhodes piano that pans left to right. And this guy claimed to be a so-called keyboardist—really, no wonder you're behind the desk! A little knowledge for these people is dangerous for the rest of us, they learn a couple of terms to be hip and they misuse them.

Figure 6.3 Sony 5003 Half-Inch Two-Track Analog Tape Machine
Erik Christian Photography

Figure 6.4 Producer Ernie McKone after dealing with Instinct Records!

When it comes down to mixing, the more you do, the better you become. Sometimes it's best to step away from a mix when you feel stuck; you get so far into it that you can't tell the trees from the forest. Believe me, a little break is good because you can come back the next day and hear it so much clearer. Ear fatigue is another thing to watch for when mixing. That's why it is important to choose a good pair of speaker monitors; each person is going to have their own opinion on them, so choose what is best for you. Choose something that is comfortable and is not going to burn you out. There will be times when the mixes fall together effortlessly and you can't believe it was that easy. However, other times it can take you days to get all of the parts to fit. I learned through experience that the easiest way to avoid difficult mixes is to plan out the tracking process and the parts you record.

No one wants to sift through hundreds of takes to find that correct two bars of music; plus, it becomes more difficult in the mix. Of course you should record a few solo tracks and some alternative parts, but just because you have the ability to record 120 tracks certainly doesn't mean you are required to do so.

Figure 6.5 Otari MTR-10 Quarter-Inch
Two-Track Analog Recorder
Erik Christian Photography

I suggest to certain adventurous souls that they warm up their mixes out of the box with a quarter-inch or half-inch analog tape machine for that final stage. It makes a big difference and will give you a fatter sound with tape compression. Plus, analog equipment has become so much more affordable, like buying an Otari MTR-10 on eBay to record your masters on. As I mentioned in Chapter 1, it is a good idea to buy some sort of sound absorption for your room to prevent any ceiling or wall reflections while mixing. Listen, you don't have to hire a sound architect; with just a bit of research online and common sense, you can adapt a room to your needs. You can even make your own baffles and absorption panels. I had some great AlphaSorb™ Barrier Fabric Wrapped Wall Panels and turned them into portable gobo/baffles on wheels.

Figure 6.6 Portable AlphaSorb™ Barrier
Fabric Wrapped Wall Panels
Erik Christian Photography

Figure 6.7 Portable wood-framed
AlphaSorb™ Barrier Fabric Wrapped
Wall Panels with wheels
Erik Christian Photography

I started with four pine boards measuring four inches wide by eight feet long and built a wood frame for each of the panels depending on the dimensions. I double sided each frame, meaning that I placed an AlphaSorb™ Barrier Fabric Wrapped Wall Panel on each side of the frame (two panels per frame), with a three-inch air gap in between them, and screwed them to the frame. Then I took a padded movers dolly and cut it in half, attaching each two-wheel section to both sides of the finished frame standing upright. After placing metal handles on each side of the frame, it became completely portable.

Figure 6.8 JBL 4410 in front of wood-
framed AlphaSorb™ Barrier Fabric
Wrapped Wall Panels
Erik Christian Photography

This is extremely useful for me, because I'm constantly moving around to different studio spaces around the country and it makes for a very easy setup. You could even make an isolation area for a drummer or horn section with this method and customize it to any size. Whether it be some small bass traps or Auralex foam on the ceiling and walls, treating the room before you mix is essential.

Figure 6.9 Studio view with portable wood-framed AlphaSorb™ Barrier Fabric Wrapped Wall Panels
Erik Christian Photography

Figure 6.10 Upright view of wood-framed AlphaSorb™ Barrier Fabric Wrapped Wall Panels
Erik Christian Photography

ANALOG MIXER VS. IN THE BOX: THE BIG ARGUMENT

Figure 6.11 Push those faders and
tweak those knobs!
Erik Christian Photography

For those of you who are new to the art of recording, there is a definite distinction between analog mixing and in-the-box or virtual mixing. Like everything, each one has its own benefits and drawbacks. But I have to say using both, at least for me, is the best way to go and is the most flexible. Analog is wonderful as I grew up strictly in an analog world of vinyl records, eight-track cassettes, compact cassettes, and then CDs. However, there were some serious negatives. In those analog days, you were limited with the equipment you had at your disposal. If you were not mixing at one of the huge recording studios like the Power Station or Ocean Way, you certainly didn't have the availability of gear. These large studios were very expensive and unless you worked there, most independent bands couldn't afford it. So a lot of us would have to go off the grid, if you will, to smaller studios with not-so-good gear to record. Nine times out of ten, the mixes sounded like rough demos, the one reason being cost! Who had the money for more studio time to fuss with a mix for days, weeks, or months? Also, a lot of us were cutting our teeth in the studio during those days, not only getting the right mixes, but also getting the right performances and compositions.

Figure 6.12 Classic compressor that no plug-in can beat!
Erik Christian Photography

I find using digital alone to be too cold and unassertive for my ears, especially when recording rock bands with live drums, bass, guitars, keys, etc. It just doesn't have the punch or the warmth. I still to this day don't like the way a live drum kit sounds recorded directly into a DAW. Of course there are hundreds of plug-ins to make it sound more like an analog signal, but why bother? If you want it to sound like analog, then record it to analog, if you don't care then just go direct. It's just like those pathetic guitar amp simulator plug-ins—gag me with a spoon. As we mentioned earlier, there are so many cheap options to record your amp in the room. Like the Line 6 amps when they came out, I tried a few and once you took off the effects of the amp it sounded like crap, this coming from a guy who has collected and recorded all types of amps for over twenty years. Anyway, digital is a very positive thing, but to get its full benefits you have to run it through some sort of analog signal going in and coming out, whether it be a summoning mixer or a traditional recording console.

The most beneficial thing about digital is its on-the-fly editing during mixing. This is perfect; if there is too much noise in a track or a wrong note, it can be fixed with a quick edit. Zakk Wylde told me that this is a great tool in the studio once he transfers all of the tracks from analog tape to Pro Tools. He can then edit verses and choruses, double sections or cut others out. Zakk said, "We recorded all analog. We'll then dump it into Pro Tools if we need to shorten it or copy and paste. Back in the day, when we recorded everything on analog, if you had to edit something, you had to cut tape and if you made a mistake, you were screwed." That's funny because there was no undo button in the analog days like on your PC or Mac of today. This is another thing to prepare for mixing—have all of your parts edited, so time is not wasted going back and finding parts to copy and paste. If there is a lot of editing to be done, I would set a specific time before mixing to get all of the parts ready so all you have to do is concentrate on the mix.

Figure 6.13 Classic Neve and Trident Compressors, EQs and Lexicon PCM 70! Erik Christian Photography

Analog EQ is a big part of why I like to mix through a recording console; no matter what plug-in you buy, it just doesn't sound the same without that three-dimensional sound. I've used virtual EQs plenty of times and they do the job, but you have to be very careful because with digital EQs you can really hurt a tone more than help it. Remember, you don't have to buy a huge console; there're a lot of smaller footprints out there by companies like Toft, Audient, Sound-craft, and Allen & Heath. Of course you can argue that the software companies keep pitching all of their new software just to make a buck. They release things that are either worthless or completely unnecessary. However, there are some great software packages available with diverse applications. Now when you consider a hardware mixer like a Neve or SSL, they are really the nerve center for the entire studio. The mix is in front of you with an analog console, mic pre-amps, and faders enabling you to multitask by EQing several tracks at once, effects sends, insert compressors to a track, etc. Mixing with the inevitable handheld mouse is just not intuitive to me; I want to be able to push up or pull down many faders at once, which is impossible with a mouse. Of course you can buy a control surface like the Artist Control surfaces by Avid, which creates a better relationship between mixer and music.

Figure 6.14 Close-up on the Trident Channels Strips
Erik Christian Photography

A typical analog channel strip found in a mixer is just like their virtual counterpart seen in Universal Audio's channel strip series, for instance. Both have a common layout that is important to understand for signal flow purposes. A typical layout is as follows:

Input Strip

Input (Microphone or Line): Trim knob control with switch to go between mic in and line in

Equalizer: Tone shaper in various frequency bands

Aux Send: Adjusts effects level on a instrument track

Pre Fader/Post Fader Switch: Adjust effects level on an instrument either before or after the fader; Post sounds close in the mix; Pre sounds far away in the mix

Channel Assign (Bus Assign): A set of switches to assign the input signal to various output channels

Solo (PFL): Allows you to hear the track by itself or with Pre Fader Listen, listen before the fader

Mute: Disables the entire channel from the mix

Phase (Polarity Invert): It switches the input polarity of the input signal 180 degrees; useful at times for stereo keyboards

Output

AUX Return: Controls the level of signal coming from the effects unit

Effects Panning: Trim knob that places the effects from left to right, wherever desired

Levels Indicators: VU or LED meters indicating signal level sent to recorder

Monitor Section

Monitor Control: Trim knob that controls the sound level in the control room

Two-Track Switch: When engaged allows you to hear program material from external two-track devices like a CD, reel to reel

MONO: Allows you to hear the monitored mix in mono, very useful to see if there are any phase issues in the mix

Figure 6.15 Trident VU
Meters with channel assign
buttons and mic/line ins
Erik Christian Photography

Now there is one thing I should point out: it took me years to collect all of the gear I have and it does come with a cost. Analog equipment has to be serviced, recapped, VU bulbs need to be replaced, tape machines need to be aligned, and this is why all the old studios used to have full-time techs on staff. When they called you an engineer, they meant it back then. If a session was interrupted by faulty gear, you were expected to know how to fix it or at the very least work around it. Remember, a lot of pressure was on an engineer in the studio with the band ready to record and the producer breathing down his neck. The engineer had to capture everything from the first take to the last, no excuses. So of course, using Pro Tools is so much easier, when all you have to do is hit the space bar to record. If you missed a punch out, who cares, you can stretch out what you just recorded over. Not only is this a very different approach to recording, but a very different philosophy all the way around.

Even if most people today are going to mix in the box, at least there are options out there that intergrade analog with virtual mixers. The truth of the matter is many of the new generation have no experience with analog, so they don't know the benefits or the difference between the two. Plus, much of the music today on the radio is recorded in the box, which makes it easy to mimic if you have the digital tools at home. It's truly a personal taste between analog and virtual mixers, as we saw in our interviews. Many of my generation who enjoyed the golden age of records were weaned on analog because it was the only thing available, but let's embrace the new age and bring some of our old techniques with us!

EFFECTS PROCESSING

Figure 6.16 MOTU Ensemble Chorus Stock with Digital Performer 8

Figure 6.17 Logic Ringshifter stock plug-in

There are countless effects processors both in the hardware and the virtual form. Every DAW system comes with a plethora of them and the hardware systems are just too numerous to name. However,

I listed below my favorite hardware outboard gear that has been on countless records around the world.

Eventide Harmonizer H3000

Figure 6.18 Eventide H3000 Ultra Harmonizer
Erik Christian Photography

This is an old-school effects processor that is a true workhorse for guitar effects. There are so many classic sounds in this unit. My particular favorite patches are H949 (one output is a straight delay and the other is a pitch-shifted delay), Micropitchshift (perfect effect to fatten up a sound—great on bass), ScaryMovie (it's a reverse-shift sound creating evil voices—awesome on guitar), Canyon (huge, sounding reverb with an echo effect—awesome for solos), Analog Delays (filtered delays with a little swept effect), and Dual H910s (this emulates two 910 units together, with left and right sides processed separately). When this processor was first released, it was very advanced and cutting edge. Today, it stands as a top guitar processor. It is also very easy to edit with the soft key function below the LED window. Every guitarist should have one.

Eventide Harmonizer GTR4000

Figure 6.19 Eventide GTR 4000 Ultra Harmonizer
Erik Christian Photography

A great effect processor developed specifically for guitar players, this Eventide has so many useful presets from the factory that can be easily tweaked and edited. There are some really fun artist patches, such as "Kill the Guy" and "Little Man" under the Steve Vai bank and "Gorgeous Delay" and "Satchelope Filter" under the Joe Satriani presets.

What's cool is that the 4000 series has a graphical editor that allows users to construct their own sound. This makes the 4000 so versatile, because the effects are made up of smaller building blocks referred to as *modules*. It's extremely useful and flexible because you can use these modules not only on your input signal, but also elsewhere in the signal chain. For example, you could use a flange on the output of a reverb. For guitar nuts like myself, this is such a cool feature because we always like to experiment with our sound.

Lexicon PCM 70

Figure 6.20 Lexicon PCM 70 Digital Effects Processor
Erik Christian Photography

We all know how wonderful the Lexicon reverb sounds, and this unit lives up to that, even though it is an old-school processor. Take, for instance, the Concert Wave preset. It really responds well to clean and bright sources like that spanking Strat sound or even a nice hollow body clean tone. The Six Across preset is a favorite because it contains six voices that are all filtered to different bandwidths and panned to different locations in the stereo field. Another nice preset is the Soft Echoes, which I usually use on acoustic guitars. It contains a reverb effect, which starts off with four discrete pre-delay echoes. Turning the soft knob control lengthens the RT times and ultimately makes the ambience brighter. It also has multi-effects, such as the Flange O Echo, Voice Combo, and Echorus; all very nice-sounding patches.

Eventide Eclipse

Figure 6.21 Eventide Eclipse Harmonizer Effects Processor
Erik Christian Photography

Yeah I know, another Eventide product. But they are an outstanding company for guitar processors. This is a modern-day Ultra Harmonizer, with some great new presets and some classic updated sounds, as well as a combination of sounds such as PitchModTrem, Ringdelays, LofoFilter, Pong, and Swampy Guitar. What is super awesome is the Tempo Tap button, which allows you to get the right BPM on the fly. It's very user friendly and intuitive. So when you load a program, all of the important parameters are located under the Hot Keys button.

Programs are made up of an effect's blocks, which you can access through the Parameters button. Each effects block runs the Eclipse's set of algorithms. This is the building block of the unit and is very easy to understand when you dig into the effects processor. When I was recording Leslie West, he really liked the program PanVerbEcho, so I wound up printing the effect separately on another track so we could use it in the mix.

MIX TIPS

Let's first talk about "unity gain" for a moment. Simply put, the input and the output levels between two devices are the same. For mixing purposes, I set the unity gain by calibrating to zero dB on the VU Meters between the mixer and the two-track device I'm recording to, like the half-inch tape, quarter-inch tape, or hard drive. Very important because you want to hear back the final two-track mix at the same audio level it was mixed. If you toggle between the two-track mix and the original mix through the desk, there should be no change in level. I do this by setting the onboard oscillator to one k and adjust

179

the stereo VU meters on the Trident mix bus to zero dB. While the two-track is on record stand-by, I set the two-track VU meters to zero dB as well; that way, the mix will play back at the same level as it was initially mixed. If the mixes are going to be mastered by a professional mastering house and you are sending analog tape, then at the beginning of the tape reel, you print what is called "tones." They would consist of one k, ten k, 100hz and any Dolby tones for thirty IPS (inches per second) and fifteen IPS tape speeds. The reason you need to send *Tone* information is because the mastering house has to align their machine to the your tape or there will be audio problems. Of course with wav files today this is unnecessary, but there are those of us who still send tapes to be mastered. A perfect working example of this is when I recently finished *Guitar for Wounded Warriors* and I sent the half-inch master analog tapes with the "tones" to a mastering house in Burbank, CA. So the engineer transferred the tapes and did a sample master on a few songs. He sent them to me and I knew right away there was something seriously wrong when I heard them. It turned out that when I was recording them, the Dolby units were lit up, but weren't engaged, so they never were encoded with Dolby. But when the mastering engineer transferred the tapes at the studio he used Dolby to decode them, which mudded the sound up. Inevitably, he had retransferred everything without Dolby and re-mastered. So if you are using analog tape, placing the proper tones on the head of the reel is super important. Probably more than you need to know and most likely you'll be sending wav files to be mastered, but good knowledge nonetheless.

BE PREPARED FOR THE MIX

- Make sure there is no hum or ground loop in your computer or hardware mixer, because that will come out in the mix.
- Have a preconceived idea of what you want to hear from the final mix.
- Have samples of the music you are trying to emulate.
- Set up a stereo channel of example music so you can compare on the fly to what you are mixing.
- Think in terms of spectral balance and stereo images.

- Use reverb and delay for a sense of distance for instruments in the mix.
- Remember, when using EQ, boosting reduces headroom compared to cutting EQ.
- Try experimenting with panning both instruments and effects.
- Always mark any fader movements, panning, mutes, and write down effects you really like, to refer to later.
- Rehearse any fader moves or panning before committing to two-track mix.
- Make sure stereo meters are *not* pinned, so as to give some headroom for mastering.
- Have more than one set of monitors to refer to during the mix, smaller and larger ones. It's a good way to see if the mix stays consistent on different speakers.
- Take breaks when you feel your ears are becoming fatigued.
- If there is an instrument solo, logical balances will bring it up in the mix and then return it to its original position once the solo is over. Nothing worse than having a solo buried.
- Frequently check the mix in mono to make sure there is no phase cancellation.
- Check mixes on headphones once in awhile to check stereo imaging.
- Download the mix as a wav file to your iPod or burn a CD and check mix in your car.
- Mix on uncolored monitors so there is no enhancement of bass or any other frequencies when mixing.
- Mix at low to medium levels; you can crank it once in a while to see how the mix holds up under loud volumes, but you don't want to burn your ears out at high levels.
- Keep the dynamics of the song. Every part of song doesn't have to blow you out of the room; some sections might be quieter than others, which is good. It is lost art in the loudness wars of recent years.
- Don't attempt to get your mixes as loud as commercial CDs simply because they have been mastered very loud and you will be unable to get those levels at home.

- If you are a producer, artist, or engineer, try to look at the mix as objectively as possible. It's hard but try to sift through the unnecessary parts and remove them. If a part is not necessary and is clouding up the mix, then get rid of it.
- Don't just pan everything either hard left, hard right, or twelve o'clock; use the other knob positions like two o'clock or nine o'clock positions. This gives a fuller stereo mix.
- Bring your instrument to the mix, just in case there is last-minute change and you want to rerecord a part or solo.
- Don't over-use EQ; if an instrument doesn't need it, then simply don't use it.
- There is no wrong way to use panning. Look at The Beatles' mixes: the drums and guitar were on one side and the bass and vocals on the other. Same with early Van Halen records where the guitar was on the left side and echoplex guitar return was on the right.
- Remember, the less reverb or delay you use on an instrument, the closer and flatter it sounds.
- If you are indecisive about a mix, record a few different versions and listen to them for a couple of days and see which one sits with you the best.
- Use some sort of buss compressor, either hardware or virtual, to control the transients and to give your mix some depth.
- If you are going to use automation, choose which type you will be using: Real Time (automates fader, pan, effects, etc., but is long procedure done in real time) or Snap Shot (performs the same thing only in intervals of the song).
- Remember that all of the parts in the song have to work together and make sense to form a good song.
- Make sure every instrument can be heard without being obtrusive.
- Subtle moves make a good mix, not noticeable, sudden fader movements. Nothing should jump right out at you from nowhere.
- Very important in the digital realm, cymbals should be crisp, but not harsh or piercing to the ear.
- Make sure the mix is clean and uncluttered without any noise or unwanted distortion.

- Make sure all the instruments are in there own frequency territory. For example, the kick drum is not masking the bass guitar because they share the same frequency range.
- Make sure there are not unwanted sibilants, S sounds in the vocal tracks.
- Give some instruments ambience and a spacious feel with effects to give the mix a depth quality.
- Make your mixes stand out with character by using such effects as flanging, echo, ring modulation, and so forth.
- Give the appropriate production to the music. For example, would you give slick production to a punk rock band? No, you want it to sound raw and rough.
- Make sure there are no lifeless-sounding tracks in your mix or it will affect the whole mix.
- Most important, never invite an A&R guy to the mix!

CONCLUSION

Mixing is the most challenging part of the recording process in the studio, because all of the work is going to be expressed in this one mix. The one thing I discovered in mixing is that it's all about listening, not just to your own mix, but also to how performances are recorded in the mix. You can't have a great mix with a drummer who is off beat or a vocalist who is out of key. I've heard good mixes with bad musicians and it just sounds bad all the way around, which makes the whole mix suck, no matter how tonally great it sounds. There have been times when I have struggled with a band that came in to record and I had to edit the crap out of their parts to make them sound halfway decent. No, I have to say a great mix has more than just pretty sounds and tonal balancing; it has to be backed up by great musicianship! Probably why I've never been a fan of pop music in general—because the musicianship, especially in the past decade, has been non-existent. Call me a snob or whatever, but it is called music, so the overall musicianship should be a very critical part. Especially with me, because I'm a guitar instrumentalist and have been for over twenty-five years, so you have to be proficient or you're out in the cold. Looks and style will only take you so far; in the end you have to be able to play your instrument. Believe me, I've played with the best of them!

Chapter 7

Business of Music

We all wanna get paid, right? Well, thanks to new technologies, today's artists can benefit from royalty streams that did not exist a short while ago. These royalties—from satellite radio and cable TV music channels, for example—are fantastic alternative ways that artists and rights holders can see income from the new digital marketplaces. In order to efficiently collect and distribute both digital and broadcast performance royalties to featured artists, musicians, and copyright holders, companies like SoundExchange, Sena, and Live Television/Videotape Supplemental Markets Fund have appeared. Many artists, however, are still not aware that money could be sitting in an account, waiting to be claimed. In the following article, I'll show, through my own experiences, how to take action to get the money that is rightfully yours.

GETTING PAID: SOUNDEXCHANGE

One of the most prominent organizations specializing in collecting digital revenue royalties is the Washington, DC–based SoundExchange, which is a non-profit Performance Rights Organization. What does SoundExchange actually do for you? Marie Farrar Knowles, Vice President of Communications explains, "SoundExchange represents the entire recorded music industry, including recording artists and record companies large and small. The licenses we administer enable digital music services to focus on what they do best, while ensuring that recording artists and record labels are compensated for their work."

Okay, so what is the organization's collection process? In other words, from whom does SoundExchange collect those royalties that are due to you?

SoundExchange collects statutory royalties from satellite radio (such as SiriusXM), Internet radio, cable TV music channels, and other outlets that stream music recordings. The organization came to prominence when a special group of copyright judges, called the Copyright Royalty Board, was appointed by the US Library of Congress to determine rates and terms for the digital performance of sound recordings. They basically named SoundExchange the sole company in the US to collect and distribute digital performance royalties on behalf of master rights owners, such as record companies and recording artists, as well as independent artists who control their own masters.

"Today," Knowles explains, "there are 2,000-plus digital radio services that leverage the license we administer to access any commercially available work. While this list is too long to share in this article, a few examples are services like iHeartRadio, Spotify Radio (mobile service), Pandora, and SiriusXM."

How considerable are the royalties? SoundExchange announced on its news page that in 2012 its total distribution to artists was $462 million, which was a historical moment for the organization. These royalties continue to increase for everyone; I've seen my own Sound-Exchange royalties grow dramatically over the years.

This royalty money, however, will not come to you automatically. In order to get the most accurate royalties, you need to provide SoundExchange with what is known as a "metadata sheet." Though it is time consuming on your part, it is extremely rewarding in the long run. Providing this key information has become a standard in the digital world. Either you or someone you hire will have to list all of your releases, as well as a comprehensive breakdown of each song's writers, publishers, track description, and album title, etc. (It's a simple Excel document.)

How important is such an organization for recording artists and record labels? Knowles states that the digital royalties SoundExchange is responsible for and the statutory license it administers is incredibly important to recording artists and record labels. "Currently," she points out, "performers in the United States are only paid when their sound recordings are performed via digital radio—they do not enjoy a full performance right. In other words, they are not compensated when their work is broadcast on AM/FM radio."

By registering with SoundExchange, the individuals who created the sound recording are now able to collect digital royalties for their work. SoundExchange does support legislation that would provide recording artists and record labels with the right to be paid royalties when their work is played via AM/FM radio. "We encourage all recording artists and labels to learn more and join us in this effort," she says.

I was so intrigued with their process because I had seen a significant increase in my own royalties. According to Knowles, in 2003, when SoundExchange became an independent non-profit organization, they were collecting royalty payments from approximately 400 digital radio services. Today, they collect and distribute royalties to artists and labels from more than 2,000 digital radio services, including satellite radio, Internet radio, and cable TV channels. This means that in just a decade, according to Knowles, "SoundExchange has put more than $1.5 billion into music creators' pockets. In fact, the organization's third-quarter 2013 payments of $153.7 million marked the highest quarterly payment to recording artists and record labels to date. When compared to SoundExchange's entire 2003 distribution of $3 million, it is clear that more and more music fans are listening to their favorite artists through digital radio."

It is important to note, as SoundExchange points out on its site, "SoundExchange is the Performance Rights Organization (PRO) for the digital age. The royalties that SoundExchange collects and distributes are for the featured artist and the sound recording copyright owner. ASCAP, BMI, and SESAC collect and distribute royalties for the songwriter, composer, and publisher. Both satellite radio providers and webcasters pay SoundExchange when they stream music due to their utilization of the statutory license."

It is still necessary, then, to join one of the three PROs: ASCAP, BMI, or SESAC, to receive your publisher and writer royalties.

LIVE TELEVISION VIDEOTAPE SUPPLE-MENTAL MARKETS FUND (LTVSMF)

Another great royalty source that I've seen grow substantially in the twenty-first century is LTVSMF. It collects and distributes residuals to musicians who have worked on live television/video productions.

Shari Hoffman, Fund Manager of the LTVSMF, explains their exact role: "We're a non-profit organization that works in association with the American Federation of Musicians (AFM) to ensure the collection, processing, and distribution of residuals to qualifying musicians who have performed music used on live television programs, such as *Saturday Night Live, The Late Show with David Letterman, The Tonight Show with Jay Leno*, various award shows (*GRAMMYS, Academy Awards, CMA Awards*, etc.), live reality programs (*American Idol, America's Got Talent, The Voice*, etc.), and the soap operas (which in the olden days were live broadcasts)."

Hoffman says the basic contract provisions that generate revenue to the Fund are the result of a collective bargaining agreement negotiated between the AFM and the major television networks and television producers in the late 1980s and early 1990s.

The actual responsibility to distribute these monies was transferred to the Film Musicians Secondary Markets Fund (FMSMF) in the late 1990s with an official "sub-fund" established to distribute monies collected for musicians working on these programs circa 2002, with a full-blown division formed in 2010 known today as the Live Television Videotape Supplemental Markets Fund.

"The provision," says Hoffman, "is that you had to have worked on at least one original AFM scoring session for a specific live television production. A live television/video production must generate some income or revenue as a result of exhibition in a supplemental market to trigger an obligation on the part of the producer/production company to contribute to the Fund."

HOW IMPORTANT IS THIS FOR THE MUSICIAN?

Can a musician expect to be paid well beyond the original airdate of a program? Hoffman asserts that many musicians receive payments far in excess of their original session payments for a program, provided that they have worked under the AFM Television Videotape Agreement. "The payments," she says, "can often continue for many years beyond the time when these programs were first produced, providing compensation for musicians and their heirs (beneficiaries) long after a musician has ceased being actively involved in recording and performing. Those who work non-union primarily get compensated only for their original session performance, and nothing else. Or, in other words, they work for a buyout."

For example, I get a check each year from the Live Television/Videotape Supplemental Markets Fund that is paid for by ABC-TV, since they own the cable station SOAPnet. This payment is for the past Union sessions I've produced for the daytime drama series *All My Children*, whose reruns are being shown on SOAPnet.

In order to get paid, there must be an AFM session contract filed with the appropriate Local for the original session(s) for the sound recording. If you ever did an AFM session for live television, this is something you need to look into because they keep a page on their website that lists names of people who have unclaimed checks with the fund.

A few years back, the payment schedule was erratic, but during the past two years the checks have become more stable, with an annual amount paid during the month of May. Though many of the soap series have been retired from the major networks, they have found a new home on cable TV and this is a great thing for the daytime composers like myself, since we all took a big hit when the majors canceled the shows.

KNOW THE DIFFERENCE

Again it is important to be clear that, like SoundExchange, the LTVSMF has its own area of focus compared to the Performance

Rights Organizations. "The PROs manage performance royalties for composers and publishers of music," adds Hoffman. "The Fund collects and distributes supplemental market payments due to musicians who performed under the AFM Television Videotape Agreement. The payments from the Fund are more of a delayed wage compensation closely related to residual payments, while payments from the PROs are royalties."

You may ask, "Hey, where does the money come from that the LTVSMF collects?" According to Hoffman, the Fund collects monies from companies that are signatory to the AFM Television Videotape Agreement. These are primarily the major television networks (ABC, CBS, and NBC), as well as the producers of the programs previously mentioned. "While the residuals come, in large part, from current programs," she says, "a large number of older programs such as *The Midnight Special*, *The Carol Burnett Show*, *The Tonight Show with Johnny Carson*, and many others also continue to pay residuals to the musicians who worked on those shows."

It is important to reiterate that the LTVSMF does not pay royalties, but rather deferred wages that come from the producer's obligation to report and pay on supplemental market revenue such as DVD sales, in-flight uses, uses on basic and standard cable, etc.

FIND OUT ABOUT NEIGHBORING RIGHTS

If you are a music performer/artist or a label owner who owns the master to commercial releases, there is another royalty stream called neighboring rights that cannot be overlooked.

All of the details and payment parameters for neighboring rights have been outlined in the 1961 Roman Convention Treaty (http://tinyurl.com/kz245pq). The convention secures protection in performances of performers, phonograms, producers of phonograms, and broadcasts of broadcasting organizations. Typically, in regards to neighboring rights, the song is split into two halves: 50 percent goes to the producers and 50 percent goes to the performer. Money is collected from radio, TV, theaters, clubs, restaurants, and various streaming sources such as web radio, satellite radio, and other digital transmissions. Plus, collections are made from private copying levies on blank recording media.

Not all countries, however, have neighboring rights representation or participate in generating royalties. Participating countries to the treaty, well over thirty in all, include Australia, Brazil, Canada, Congo, France, Germany, Great Britain, and Japan. (See the above link for a complete list.)

Since the United States is not included on this list, it can be a bit tricky for American artists. For an American artist to be eligible, the music must have been recorded in one of the participating countries. Lucky for me, some of my releases on Instinct Records are eligible because I recorded them in England, a country that is part of the neighboring rights pact.

So if you recorded or mastered your CD in one of the participating countries, you qualify as well. Complicated, yes, but it is the reality. I looked into various companies out there to collect these royalties for me, but unfortunately, for obvious reasons, America does not have many.

SENA

After doing copious research, I joined the Dutch society, simply known as Sena (http://sena.nl), to collect for me worldwide. Sena grants licenses on behalf of the rights holders to companies or organizations that use music, and then collect the associated fees. Sena also monitors and registers where, how, and with what purpose music is played, to get the appropriate license.

Does this sound familiar? Well, it should, because they are a lot like the PROs except they handle the rights of the master holders and the performers. I wish America had a domestic society like this. The closest we have is SoundExchange.

Whom does Sena represent?

Sena grants licenses on behalf of the rights holders to companies that use music, and they collect the associated fees. Sena, additionally, monitors and registers where, how, and with what purpose music is played. Then they distribute the royalties correctly to their producers and artists. As a neighboring rights society, Sena represents Phil Collins, Coldplay, The Beatles, The Rolling Stones, Mumford & Sons, Black Eyed Peas, and Christina Aguilera. Like our American PROs, Sena has the laborious task of inspecting playlists from radio and television stations.

Sena abides by The Dutch Neighbouring Rights Act of 1993, which gives performing artists, film/record companies, and broadcasting organizations the right to decide whether a performance may be recorded, reproduced or broadcast, shown or played. They have what is called a "right to payment," which allows commercially released music to be broadcast, with the stipulation of a reasonable fee being paid.

I'm so pleased to know they enforce that "failure to comply with the Neighbouring Rights Act is a punishable offence." Hell, if they enforced that in the US, two-thirds of the country would be punished.

A FINAL WORD ON ROYALTY COMPANIES

As an indie artist, it is important to be involved with all of these companies, so you can enjoy all of your future royalties. As we know, royalties do not always get paid to the appropriate person, but that does not mean you should just sit and let it happen. You have to actively search them out and get the right companies to represent your music.

I actually found out about royalties Sena was holding for me when I was contacted by a Dutch sub-publisher via email. He wanted to collect them on my behalf (how sweet), but for an outrageous fee of 50 percent! Absolutely ridiculous! So I contacted Sena directly, joined, and got paid royalties owed.

One of the most important pieces of advice I can give anyone about any royalty source is to be sharp and on your game. Soak up as much knowledge about it as you can.

Questions are your friend.

WHAT YOU SHOULD KNOW ABOUT LICENSING MUSIC

Throughout these tumultuous times for the music industry, one thing has remained constant—the lucrative fees in broadcast and film licensing. These fees can range anywhere from hundreds of dollars to tens of thousands of dollars and, in some cases, additional reuse fees. To get your music placed, it really comes down to hitting the pavement, shaking hands, and making phone calls to build contacts. Here's what works for me.

1. Use resource guides

I've always found that resource guides are a good place to start making connections. Having more than one guide or directory is even better—you can cross-reference them. The Music Registry publishes a host of reference guides for the music industry, like the *Film & Television Music Guide* and the *Music Publisher Registry*. They were one of the first companies to tackle this type of directory for TV and film music contacts back in the early '90s. What is most impressive about this guide is that it carries pertinent information about music supervisors, music editors, music departments, etc. There are other resources, too, like the *Hollywood Creative Directory*, *411 Directories*, and the *Blu-Book Directory* that are available, but *The Music Business Registry* is still the most thorough of its kind. And do not forget that *Music Connection*, which is well known for its guides and directories, is always updated annually.

2. Do your homework

Once you have a list of contacts to approach, make sure your music is appropriate to submit to these particular contacts. Meaning, if you are a pop vocalist, make sure that these people you are contacting actually license vocal music and not just sixty-second promo instrumental music or blues. The best way to research this is to first watch the shows in question and make note of their likes and styles, so when you contact them you sound well informed. Also before making cold calls, try to get a referral from someone they know. How do you do that? If the contact person is not able to use your music, *always* ask them whom they can recommend. If they are able to give you a name, then you know you can use that person's name for a referral to make the new contact. Keep a detailed log as well. Write down the date you spoke to a contact and any other pertinent information, such as he or she "told me to call back in June to follow up on a new show."

3. Build a catalog

Product—that's what you need! When you start shopping your music for licensing possibilities, have at least a CD worth of material. It seems fruitless when people shop only one song to a music supervisor, unless it's a huge hit from an artist that everyone knows, like Lady Gaga. Sure, there is always a possibility that one song could be perfect for a scene and they could license it, but if you are going to all this trouble to contact people, it just makes sense to have a number of tracks to shop to get a fighting chance. Especially in today's digital revolution, you can put tons of music on thumb drives and mail it off.

4. Pick the right contacts

It will save a lot of time if you make preliminary calls to the music departments to see if they, in fact, license music from outside contributors. Certain companies have exclusive licenses with music libraries and are restricted in using outside sources. Also there are certain shows that don't license outside music and only use one music composer for the show. Please keep in mind that a lot of your success is determined by timing and whether or not a show needs your type of music.

When speaking with the music supervisor, always try to see what kind of music they may need in upcoming episodes, attempt to gauge what their future licensing needs are, and inquire if they are developing other projects—if they can't use one of your songs now, they may be able to use it in the future.

5. Understand music libraries

A common question I get is, "What is a music production library?" Simply, they are music companies, like First Com, Megatrax, Sonoton, etc., who hire composers to produce music that's affordable for all sorts of broadcast and film productions. So if a show wants a pop vocal song and can't afford licensing a track by Rihanna from Def Jam, they go to a place like Killer Tracks and license a sound-alike. It's pretty straightforward and simple for productions because these libraries own both the masters and the sync (publishing), so it's a one-stop shop.

In the new millennium, there has become a new business model for these libraries, places like Crucial Music, Pump Audio, and Rumble Fish, where these companies aren't hiring composers to build their catalog, but instead licensing tracks from a plethora of musicians out there and offering the songs up for licensing.

6. Check out *The Hollywood Reporter*

This is the classic guide for TV and film people through the decades. Thing is, it is also a great resource for music placement contacts. They offer nice online access to both TV and film productions, with the specific production data, like phone numbers and addresses. This resource doesn't offer music supervisor information, so you have to call the main production number for each listing and ask them for the appropria fans. Understand the te music contact. This is where cross referencing with your other directories comes into play; sometimes people are reluctant to give emails or numbers over the phone, so as long as you have a full name, you can look it up. More than likely you'll find the detailed information you need.

7. Target music editors

While a music supervisor is more of an administrator, licensing the music from the various sources, a music editor physically places the music in the shows. A lot times music editors may *temp* in a piece of music and it will wind up staying in the show as a final. It is good then for editors to have your music on hand so it's immediately available to be placed. In the past, I've had a lot of success like this and it has sometimes turned into a productive business relationship. Some will even call on you personally to compose original score for them down the line.

As with music supervisors, the best way to connect with music editors is to reach out by phone and see if they are open to using outside source music and are able to license directly from artists. They can also refer you to the music supervisor they are working with on current shows. This goes for post-production facilities as well. You can contact post supervisors at the various houses and see if they are in a position to license music directly. Like editors, they drop in music at the last minute if a scene is not working. Access to your music is key for these people to place it in their productions.

GOING FOR A COMPOSING CAREER

There is more to composing than just buying a computer and a handful of plug-ins! After twenty years composing for television and films, with three Emmys and seven nominations, I've come to rely on instincts and input from producers and music editors around me. It's a team effort, and the sooner you learn this lesson, the better.

1. Get the vibe

Remember, you are composing music for the show, which will be heard by its fans. Understand the viewers and what works between score and picture. In Ken Burns's *Civil War* series, what worked was that beautiful solo violin melody, not blazing metal guitar. Proper background score is a key to a successful series.

2. Understand exactly what the producer or music supervisor wants

This can be a very tricky thing. It can change from day to day and from moment to moment. I found that it could become confusing if more than one person gives you directions. The best thing to do is ask for musical references from the main person giving the instructions. For example, if they are requesting a vibe like Led Zeppelin-meets-Metallica, then make sure you get your project's creative team to specify what elements of each band they like and how they want them combined. Ask as many questions as possible to nail the exact vibe they want.

3. Don't rush it—take time and get it right

This really pertains to composing for new clients. Even if you are juggling many projects, as we all seem to do, give it the time it deserves. Clients can sense when you are rushing and not giving it the proper attention. Remember the kids in school who had six weeks to do their final paper, but waited until the night before to do it? By showing the client that you care about their project, it will almost ensure you a continued relationship for future projects.

4. Use real instruments when you can, don't rely on plug-ins and sample CDs

As a guitarist and recording artist for many years, I find it annoying that there are so many electronic composers today who take the shortcut and substitute talent for computer plug-ins and samples. Instead of getting a real drummer, they use some drum "extraordinaire" plug-in and samples from CDs of horns and bass. It makes no sense—just hire real musicians to make it sound as authentic as possible. Back in the day, I remember laboring through sessions getting musicians to nail the right sound before the digital era and plug-ins; it actually was a great challenge to see if you could achieve the sound for the project and a real feeling of reward when you did.

197

5. Don't reuse old cues

This is something we are all guilty of—yours truly as well! In all my experience, I've found that trying to rework old cues to make them sound different for a new client is more time-consuming than actually composing from scratch. And trying to pass off an old cue to a new client thinking it's "close enough" is bad business, because nine out of ten times, the client will have so many changes that you will be doubling your work. I don't know how many guys do this, but it's a lot like trying to turn a polka song into an electronica tune and passing it off to the client. Believe me, they will know!

6. Watch the show and understand how the music is used

Believe it or not, there are composers out there who do not bother to watch the show they are composing for, which seems like a recipe for failure. Set your DVR to record a few episodes and see how the music is synced to picture and compose accordingly. Before I even start composing for a new show I always watch a number of episodes and then go back to the music director and ask what specifically worked for those shows in regards to the music. I also like to throw out ideas to the music director before I proceed, to see if I'm on track.

7. Make sure to send WAV samples (no MP3s) for approval

I've learned not to send MP3s to people, because no matter how many times you explain to them that it's an MP3, they always get bothered about it sounding "too compressed and lacking bottom end." Well, that's because *it's an MP3* and you're listening to it on *computer speakers!!!* Then of course they look at the file size and say, "Oh, okay then, never mind." So there goes a half-hour of my life I won't get back!

8. Never send a demo sample!

Man, this is such a catch-22, you wouldn't believe! Clients always say just send a demo so I can hear how it's coming along. So you send a rough mix to them and the first thing they say is, "It sounds like a demo!" Well *duh*, it *is* a demo! So if you are going to play something for anyone for the first time, it should be the final mix of the song. Back in the early days of being a recording artist I remember the record label would always tell me to just send demos or rough mixes of the songs "so we can get an idea of what you are working on." These were the days before I had a nice recording studio; my setup was just a Tascam DA-88 and a cheap Carvin mixer. So off the rough mixes went and the label would come back with, "It sounds like a demo!" Well yeah, that's because they are demos that you said were okay to send!

9. Keep in good communication with the producer or music supervisor

This is one of the most important things to do. Always check in with the client, especially if you have a long lead-time for the final deadline, because ideas can change. For example, that song they told you to emulate at the start of the project may have changed three times and the client might have forgotten to tell you. Of all my advice to you, this is the most crucial! I've been involved in projects that started off as heavy metal then midway became techno and then finally wound up as a punk song I had to compose from scratch. Yes, it's a lot of work and chasing, but it's all part of the gig.

10. Never say, "That's the best I can do!"

Many of us have been at the end of our rope with certain clients, for one reason or another—you want to say, "I'm done, you do it!" I certainly have been there with a few people, but the best thing to do is ask for an extension if the changes they request become too much.

Step away from the project for a few days, if possible, then come back to it with fresh ears and appease the client.

SELLING ROYALTIES

Are you an artist who has considered selling his old music catalog and still make money from it? Everyone seems to know something of the value of selling their publishing, but not everyone recognizes the intricacies of selling their writer's royalties. I must have Googled this topic a hundred times, but there really is very little information out there. I believe it is such a specialized topic, that few people have traveled down this road. I've done research in the past couple years, however, and found out some enlightening things. For one, the writer's royalty share of, say, ASCAP, SESAC, and BMI can be a very valuable commodity to outside investors. Because of the huge swings in the stock and real estate markets, more and more investors, both independent and corporate, are venturing into attaining entertainment royalties, which don't fluctuate during recessions. But with the good comes the bad. I want artists to be aware of whom to steer away from and what is a sensible deal. So read on if you're interested in some friendly advice for artists who want to earn money from old catalogs.

Understand Breakdown of Royalties to Sell

You should understand that a song has two sides as far as public performance royalties go. Those are collected by what is commonly referred to as PROs (Performance Rights Organizations) in the United States—ASCAP, BMI, SESAC. Now you have writers' and publishers' sides that are valued the same, as far as royalties paid by the PROs. In other words, if a song is placed on a daytime TV show and earns $130 for the writer, then the publisher side of this song for the same placement will earn the same amount.

So from the standpoint of the performance royalties, they are basically of equal value (don't confuse this with sync fees or mechanical royalties). Even if you don't control the publishing side of the song or even the copyright, you can still sell your writer royalty stream.

For example, say you have a catalog of songs that have been earning an average of 25k per year; the common sales multiple is usually four to five times the average. Hence this catalog would be worth 100k to 125k. There are some companies/individuals that may value the catalog a little higher or lower depending on the intrinsic value they put on the catalog, for example, hit songs, television themes, etc. At the end of the day, it really depends on how eager an investor is to acquire the catalog.

Know the Sales Breakdown

Generally there are two ways of earning money on your catalog:
- An advance against future royalties
- The actual sales of your royalties

There are a couple of ways the advance works. One is when a company will offer a modest advance, usually no more than the total yearly income. They collect 100 percent of your writer's catalog until the advance is recouped, plus a very high interest rate. Investment bank companies have been known to offer high advances plus a high interest rate, and then take 50 percent of the writer's side for life.

I have been offered this type of deal and advise to keep clear of it because they are not buying that 50 percent of your writer's side, just giving you an advance/loan and will collect the advance 100 percent until recouped—plus hitting you with a high interest rate (in the 20 percent range) while taking 50 percent of your writer's side. Absolutely ridiculous! The only way this model would work is if the large advance was put towards the purchase of the 50 percent writer's share and was not recoupable. Hence from that point forward they collect 50 percent of the writer's.

My advice is the second option—selling the catalog outright. It is the best and quickest way to make money from your older catalog (for the right price, of course). Plus, you don't have to sell 100 percent of your writer's share either; you may only want to sell 25 percent or even 10 percent, but keep in mind the purchase price will drop with the smaller percentages. You have no "so-called" investment partners with the buy-out model and you are not obligated to pay back an advance via recoupment, which in some cases leaves you liable for the un-recouped amount if not paid back within a period of time.

PERFORMANCE RIGHTS ORGANIZATIONS

Performance Rights Organizations (PROs) are a very important part of the puzzle in the music world. Simply, each country or territory has a PRO and here in America we are blessed to have three to choose from: SESAC, ASCAP, and BMI. These companies represent hundreds of thousands of copyrights and issue licenses to users like broadcast stations, radio, cable, etc. They then collect the monies from the users and pay their affiliates. What I've found in twenty years is that everyone has his or her own experiences with each society, which can be drastically different from case to case. I prefaced this chapter with writing about my actual life experiences with these societies through the last twenty years. Now you can speak to other people with completely different perspectives. You can also call each one of these companies and speak with a writer relationship person that will BS you all day on how great they are, but the real question is how do they behave under fire? The following is my reality and what I have found.

ASCAP

When I first started composing for music production libraries many moons ago, no one told me there was a choice in which organization to use. The guy I was working with at the time told me to just call ASCAP, I couldn't pronounce the name let alone know what they did. So like many young composers, I requested a membership application, opened up a publishing company and joined as a composer, having absolutely no idea what the hell to expect. Well the next years were certainly eye opening, to say the least. I noticed that as my catalog grew and I received more airplay, the ASCAP statements seemed to be written in some sort of secret code, especially when it came to foreign royalties. Every quarter when I received the statement, I would sit down and try to make sense of the statements. This is why I always requested cue sheets from shows whenever possible, so I could at least cross reference the cue sheets with the statements. Inevitably, there was always a show payment missing or an underpayment. Every quarter I was on the phone with a representative that knew far less than I did about how it worked. I remember finally one representative saying to me, "You can't expect to get paid for every airing!" Well, hells yeah! The running joke with members at ASCAP was, "It wasn't caught in our survey," because they would all say that when they couldn't explain how the monitoring system worked. I felt like saying to this lady, "How about if your boss comes down to your little cubical in the corner of your stuffy midtown office and tells you casually, "I can't pay you this week, because your hours weren't caught in our survey." I bet that would make you think twice! This is why I always had problems with music administrative people in the industry.

They break your balls when you try to find out the simplest things about your artist catalog, while giving you attitude on the other end of the phone. They barely know their own job, and what they don't realize is that some of us actually make a living composing music and deserve to be treated with respect, not contempt. This is not just ASCAP, mind you, it can be a host of other paper-pushing workers in various companies, in industries such as publishing, record labels, marketing, radio, etc. Anyway, this is when I realized that I had to take charge of my royalties and educate myself on how it worked. Unfortunately, a lot of musicians prefer not to take a proactive stance when it comes to the business side of music. I don't blame them; it is the other side of the brain that we don't like venturing into if we can help it. It can be very uncomfortable dealing with all of these admin people and challenging them at their own game. To be honest, that's why I'm writing this book, to help fellow musicians overcome this challenge and become more knowledgeable in this subject. So the next time you speak to your PRO or to a production company, ask more questions and don't be afraid to say no if you do not accept their terms.

Unfortunately, ASCAP is also behind in technology and always has been. I remember in the late '90s befriending a guy who worked in the radio department as a musicologist; in fact, he knew of me because the radio hits I had at the time—that's a nice ego boost. ASCAP would place him, along with a host of other people, in a large room with cubicles containing headphones and cassette players at each desk. They would listen and decipher tapes that were recorded on location of radio broadcasts around the country. Typically, there were guys in vans at different US marketplaces that would sit and record hours of radio formats and then physically mail them back to the ASCAP headquarters in Lincoln Center. Excuse me, but we are on the brink of the twenty-first century, are you kidding me? This is the technology you used thirty years ago and you can't find another, more modern way to monitor radio—ever heard of BDS? I couldn't believe it until he took me up to his office and showed me the setup. Holy smokes, I was convinced that ASCAP really was trying to avoid moving forward. What a waste of manpower and money to pay for crews to go out on location and a team of people to decipher the music. They since were forced to abandon the system and go with BDS. Talk about wasting affiliates' money; this was the poster child for it.

BMI

I do have publishing companies with all three societies, which is a great way to compare payments, especially if you have a song that is split with two or more societies. Which leads me to my next story, this time about BMI. I had a number of radio hits back in the '90s in the NAC format, which later became Smooth Jazz. One of my songs, "One Arabian Knight" released by *Instinct Records*, charted #4 on R&R/ Gavin radio charts when there was such a thing. There were two other writers with me on the song and the song was split between BMI and ASCAP. I controlled 100 percent of the publishing and collected performances through both societies on the publisher side. After comparing the statements between ASCAP and BMI, it was clear that BMI barely even acknowledged the format, at least in royalty payments. For every $500 that ASCAP paid, BMI only paid $50 for the exact same song and the same publisher splits—meaning that the two other writers had 15 percent each on the song and I had 70 percent. Now between those two writers, one being BMI and the other ASCAP, BMI only paid 10 percent of what ASCAP paid for the same airplay and percentage. No trick mirrors or brain surgery, BMI was screwing the other writer and my publishing company. So as I have always done in my life, I picked up the phone and called BMI, I proceeded to be transferred from every goddamn office from L.A. to Nashville to New York. I additionally mailed (this was before the email generation) them the ASCAP statement and the BMI statement as proof.

Finally after weeks of trying, I got through to some dumbass secretary to the VP of writers' affairs. I explained the whole story to her and her response was, "I've never heard of that song before!" Houston, we've got a problem . . . beam me up, Scotty! I don't believe I asked you if you were familiar with song; in fact, I only asked to speak to your boss! This is the kind of stuff we're all up against! Bottom line, I did in fact speak to her boss later, who was dumbfounded that I would ask such a question. Finally, he just had to admit that BMI didn't care about this format (NAC), put very little resources in monitoring these radio stations and yes, the old cliché, "it wasn't caught in our survey." Ironically, around this time BMI had in place a policy they advertised to members that they would match payments in these types of instances with what ASCAP paid. I bet you know what happened next? BMI weaseled out of it and said they no longer honored that policy. I have no use for people like this, so it was time to move forward and make sure to learn from these experiences.

SESAC

When I moved over to SESAC, I knew things were going to be much different and they were. First off, SESAC is a privately owned, for-profit organization, whereas ASCAP and BMI are non-profit organizations and are bound to a consent decree. Basically, ASCAP and BMI have certain restrictions they have to abide by on court settlements concerning antitrust problems. So clearly, SESAC has much more flexibility as a company and in court negotiations. In fact, SESAC was just sold in 2013 to a private equity firm for $600 million. Hey, there is absolutely nothing wrong with being a for-profit organization; truthfully, this is what drives American businesses. I believe that with the sale, SESAC's affiliates will benefit greatly. I've spoken to several board members of ASCAP and they think it's sacrilegious to be a for-profit PRO company. I say piss off! Let me tell you that ASCAP is trying to keep the masses ignorant! Look who sits on the board of ASCAP and the president, all Tin Pan Alley writers from the Brill building days of music publishing. The fact of the matter is that those songs do not constitute the majority of music licenses any longer and haven't for a long time. It's already been proven years ago that 80–85 percent of the music broadcasted over all media is background source music and themes. But if you have the older generation that benefits from the status quo, who have special interests in the current royalty system, well hell they aren't about to change it and take money out of their royalty-lined pockets. It's like expecting congress to voluntarily ask for a pay cut; it's just not going to happen. As I was coming up through the ranks this was eye opening, man!

Now back to SESAC, there a few important things that make them stand out. They have quite a large catalog now because of the catalog acquisitions of Bob Dylan, Neil Diamond, Rush, and television composers like Bruce Miller and Jonathan Wolf. For one, their reps are very easy to talk to and discuss any types of royalty issues. For instance, like the BMI issue I mentioned earlier, I had a similar situation occur when I was writing for daytime television. SESAC's daytime rate was lower than ASCAP's; I brought it to their attention, showed them the ASCAP statement and the SESAC statement as proof and you know what, they matched the royalty fee for that airplay and any future royalties! Now that is what I'm talking about, R-E-S-P-E-C-T! Finally a PRO that get its! There was no chasing or arguing, I simply showed them the situation and they made good. Also, when the watermark and monitor system of Verance closed down, they continued to pay me an average every quarter, based on what I was making when the system was running, indefinitely until another system was developed to replace it. These people went above and beyond any PRO I ever worked with.

Technology is a topic where SESAC soars head and shoulders above the other two. They are always trying out new ways to get the affiliates paid faster and more accurately. One of the large reasons I went to SESAC back in the late '90s was because they had partnered in a new technology that involved watermarking music. This to me was such a fantastic idea I couldn't believe no one had come up with it sooner. The idea was to digitally place an inaudible watermark on a piece of music so it could be detected anywhere if used in broadcasting, as well as under a voiceover or buried in the mix of a television show. Once Verance, the company who was monitoring and issuing the watermark, got up and running I have to tell you it worked damn well! Verance in turn would supply the monitoring details to SESAC to pay their affiliates accordingly. My SESAC statements literally went from being fifteen pages to being over a thousand pages, I kid you not! It contained all kinds of detections from every small local station to major networks and cable channels. The first thing I did was watermark my commercial releases and library CDs I composed/produced for Megatrax, FirstCom, and Sonoton. The only drawback was since music had to have a physical watermark placed in it, you couldn't redo music that was already released, unless you were doing a second pressing. Also it's worth noting that for the everyday composer like myself, I couldn't send the music to get watermarked at Verance when I was doing daily and weekly shows. However, since I was writing for major networks, I wasn't worried about the watermark for them, it was the local markets that were troublesome. I'm convinced that the local markets do not bother to create cue sheets or hassle with submitting paperwork to the PROs. They think music is free and anyone can use it as they see fit. Some at least abuse the rules of engagement to an extent. It's mostly with library music, where the watermark became so useful. Case in point, I heard a number of songs that I composed for FirstCom on a Fox

Sports channel, so I recorded it. I contacted FirstCom who in turn contacted the channel to look into this claim. I even sent them the actual video with the music.

First, Fox didn't even have the cue sheets for the shows, then when put on the spot by FirstCom they made one up out of the blue, just grabbing any library CDs on the shelf, except for the ones they really played of course, just to appease FirstCom. If we had the watermarking system working at the time, it would have been there in black and white on the detection report. The major networks like ABC, CBS, and NBC are very diligent in submitting cue sheets to the PROs, so there's never a real big issue. By the way, for those of you who don't know, a cue sheet is a document created by the user, network, cable station, etc., which lists all music used within a particular television program, movie, or mini-series. It contains all of the pertinent information about the music, such as song title, writer/publisher information, song duration, and how the music is used, as a theme or in the background. Unfortunately, because of costly lawsuits and monitoring systems, Verance abandoned the project only after a couple years. SESAC went on to try another failed watermarking system and is currently using a fingerprint technology like BDS. However, they have not found one that has the same far-reaching success into the local markets as Verance, but here's hoping the future brings success. It is worth noting that both ASCAP and BMI refused to pay affiliates from Verance who supplied monitoring data and that SESAC was the only PRO that paid on this system. In fact, ASCAP and BMI bought their own watermark technology and never did anything with them. I believed they only bought these technologies to sit on them so no one else would use them, but never had plans in actually putting them to use. Again the board members who run ASCAP and BMI, who are old singer/songwriters, certainly don't want to use a technology that will certify what everyone has known for years and decrease their own royalties.

Ultimately, it is your decision in the end which PRO you choose to represent your works. I always loved the story a former president of SESAC told me, about when Bob Dylan resigned from ASCAP and took his whole catalog over to SESAC. Dylan did not even receive a farewell phone call from ASCAP asking him to reconsider his decision. I, on the other hand, got a call from ASCAP before I left; that's crazy! I figured the kids at ASCAP at the time had no idea that Dylan's legal name was Robert Zimmerman, so it slipped right by them at a costly price! It was a good thing for SESAC affiliates that Dylan and Diamond came over, because it really put SESAC on the map and more importantly it gave them negotiating leverage for the radio and television licenses, especially with the Television Music Licensing Committee (TMLC). Now TMLC can't say they don't play any SESAC artists, so they have to pony up to the table with decent license fees, a real turning point for SESAC. The other thing you have to understand is that by decree ASCAP and BMI have to accept every applicant, whereas SESAC, being a private company, can pick and choose their affiliates. ASCAP has 450,000 members and BMI 550,000 while SESAC is small in comparison, only a few thousand members. But being a very selective society, it gets the cream of the crop! One thing to keep in mind, if you are a current member of ASCAP or BMI, if you ever decide to resign, make sure to read over the rules and regulations on how to proceed. Both societies have a very small window of opportunity for when you can actually resign. ASCAP is yearly in September, on specific dates, and if you miss it, you will have to wait another year before you can leave. Also, it is better to leave your catalog there because if you take it, they will refuse to pay you the last six months of royalties, putting them into the slush fund. Upon my resignation, I instructed ASCAP to continue to represent my catalog, starting fresh with new material at SESAC. BMI plays a similar game where if you miss the resignation date, you're renewed automatically, for another two to five years, depending on their current licenses with broadcasters. So be very punctual if you want to move to another PRO.

Appendix

HIGHLY RECOMMENDED READING

*Introduction to Professional Record-
ing Techniques*
by Bruce Bartlett
Howard W. Sams & Company
(1988)

Microphones, Third Edition
by Martin Clifford
Tab Books Inc. (1986)

Behind the Glass
by Howard Massey
Backbeat Books (2000)

Producing in the Home Studio
by David Franz
Berklee Press (2001)

*Sound Studio Construction on a
Budget*
by F. Alton Everest
McGraw Hill (1997)

*Home Recording for Musicians for
Dummies*, Fourth Edition
by Jeff Strong
John Wiley & Sons (2012)

*Home Recording Studio: Build It
Like the Pros*
by Rod Gervais
Cengage Learning

PRO AUDIO MANUFACTURERS

Sure Microphones
5800 West Touhy Avenue
Niles, IL 60714-4608 Toll Free
(US only)
(800) 25-SHURE (800-257-4873)
info@shure.com
www.shure.com

Neumann USA
1 Enterprise Drive

Old Lyme, CT 06371
Tel.: +1 (860) 434-9190
Fax: +1 (860) 434-1759
neumann-help@neumannusa.com
www.neumannusa.com

Rupert Neve Designs
P.O. Box 1969
Wimberley, TX 78676
512-847-3013

info@rupertneve.com
www.rupertneve.com

Avid/Pro Tools
Pacific Plaza Bldg,
2001 Junipero Serra Blvd,
Daly City, CA 94014-3886
Tel: 650-731-6300
www.avid.com

Apple/Logic
1 Infinite Loop
Cupertino, CA 95014
408-996-1010
www.apple.com

Spectrasonics
P.O. Box 7336
Burbank, California 91510
818-955-8481
info@spectrasonics.net
www.spectrasonics.net

Arturia USA
5776-D Lindero Cyn Rd., #239
Westlake Village, CA 91362
info@arturia.com
www.arturia.com

MOTU
1280 Massachusetts Ave
Cambridge, MA 02138
617-576-2760
www.motu.com

Slate Digital
323-656-2050
sales@stevenslate.com
www.slatedigital.com

Universal Audio, Inc.
4585 Scotts Valley Dr.
Scotts Valley, CA 95066
877-698-2834
sales@uaudio.com
www.uaudio.com

Pulse Techniques, LLC
PO Box 271669
Fort Collins, CO 80527-1669
888-478-5832
www.pulsetechniques.com

BAE Audio
7421 Laurel Canyon Blvd.,
   Unit 14
N. Hollywood, CA 91605
818-784-2046
contact-us@baeaudio.com
www.baeaudio.com

DBX
10653 South River Front Park-
   way, Suite 300
South Jordan, UT 84095
801-566-8800
support@dbxpro.com
www.dbxpro.com

Purple Audio
16 W Broadway
Jim Thorpe, PA 18229
718-482-8494
purple@purpleaudio.com
www.purpleaudio.com

JDK Audio
JDK Audio c/o API
8301 Patuxent Range Road
Jessup, MD 20794
301-776-7879

www.JDKAudio.com
Solid State Logic
sales@solidstatelogic.com
www.solidstatelogic.com

AMS Neve Ltd
AMS Technology Park
Billington Road
Burnley BB11 5UB, England
+44 (0)1282 457 011
info@ams-neve.com
www.ams-neve.com

TRADE MAGAZINES

Mix
NewBay Media, LLC
1111 Bayhill Drive, Suite 440
San Bruno, CA 94066
www.mixonline.com

Pro Sound News
NewBay Media, LLC.
28 East 28th Street, 12th Floor,
New York, NY 10016
www.prosoundnetwork.com

Sound On Sound
Media House
Trafalgar Way, Bar Hill,
Cambridge, CB23 8SQ, United
  Kingdom.
+44 (0)1954 789888
www.soundonsound.com

Tape Op
www.tapeop.com

WEB REFERENCES

AES (Audio Engineering Society)
www.aes.org

Home Recording Forum
www.homerecording.com

Copyright Office on Audio
  Home Recording
www.copyright.gov/
  title17/92chap10
Audio Home Recording Act

wp.aarcroyalties.com/ahra

Pro Sound Web
www.prosoundweb.com/article/
print/can_grammy_winning_
recordings_be_made_in_a_
home_studio/

Mix Online
www.mixonline.com/ms/aes/vid-
eos/studio_visit_brian_tarquin/

Music Connection Recording
Tips
www.musicconnection.com/
expert-advice-recording-tips-
indie-artist/

Recording History With Deep
Purple
www.deep-purple.am/machine_
head_album_history_en.html

Andy Johns Recordings
www.uaudio.com/blog/artist-
interview-andy-johns/

Roy Thomas Baker Recording
Queen
www.youtube.com/
watch?v=ZidiPxbgg8Q

Rick Rubin Producing Black
Sabbath
www.youtube.com/
watch?v=p6h6bUVZbDo

Bob Rock Legendary Producer
www.youtube.com/
watch?v=_674vq3x-HQ

Jimmy Page: Recording at
Headley Grange
www.youtube.com/
watch?v=KWI9bMe7gHE

Andy Johns Interview on
Producing
www.youtube.com/
watch?v=ptDRJ6Vyelg

James Taylor & Yo-Yo Ma
Recording
www.youtube.com/
watch?v=Fb5ZyPH41vE

Index

Books from Allworth Press

Allworth Press is an imprint of Skyhorse Publishing, Inc. Selected titles are listed below.

Booking Performance Tours: Marketing and Acquiring Live Arts and Entertainment
by Tony Micocci (paperback, 6 x 9, 304 pages, $24.95)

Guitar Encyclopedia
by Brian Tarquin (paperback, 8 ½ x 11, 256 pages, $29.95)

How to Grow as a Musician: What All Musicians Must Know to Succeed
by Sheila E. Anderson (paperback, 6 x 9, 256 pages, $25.50)

Making and Marketing Music: The Musician's Guide to Financing, Distributing, and Promoting Albums
by Jodi Summers (paperback, 6 x 9, 240 pages, $19.95)

Making it in the Music Business
by Lee Wilson (paperback, 6 x 9, 256 pages, $24.95)

Managing Artists in Pop Music: What Every Artist and Manager Must Know to Succeed
by Mitch Weiss and Perri Gaffney (paperback, 6 x 9, 288 pages, $23.95)

Profiting from Your Music and Sound Project Studio
by Jeffrey Fisher (paperback, 6 x 9, 224 pages, $24.95)

The Quotable Musician: From Bach to Tupac
by Sheila E. Anderson (paperback, 7.6 x 7.6, 224 pages, $19.95)

Rock Star 101: A Rock Star's Guide to Survival and Success in the Music Business
by Marc Ferrari (paperback, 176 pages, $17.95)

The Songwriter's and Musician's Guide to Nashville
by Sherry Bond (paperback, 6 x 9, 256 pages, $19.95)

Starting Your Career as a Musician
by Neil Tortorella (paperback, 6 x 9, 240 pages, $19.95)

Insider's Guide to Music Licensing
by Brian Tarquin (paperback, 6 x 9, 256 pages, $19.95)

To see our complete catalog or to order online, please visit *www.allworth.com*.